In A Cloud of Sails

Canada's forgotten Lady of the Sea

by

George Opacic

and

Ron M. Craig

copyright © Ron M. Craig and George Opacic 2018

Authors: George Opacic and Ron M. Craig

Publisher: Rutherford Press
rutherfordpress.ca

For information, contact:

Rutherford Press
PO Box 648
Qualicum Beach, BC, V9K 1A0 Canada
info@rutherfordpress.ca
https://rutherfordpress.ca

Printed in the United States of America and Canada

All rights reserved. No part of this book may be reproduced in whole or in part, materially or digitally, including photocopying, without the express written permission of the authors or publisher.

ISBN (paperback) # 978-0-9951743-7-5

ISBN (ebook) # 978-0-9951743-8-2

Book design by George Opacic

Figures/illustrations copyright of the authors or as noted.

DEDICATION

To my Father, Ron Sr. The most interesting man
I have ever known!

This book is dedicated to Ron C. Craig and to each
of the people who built and sailed the
Monte Cristo / Endeavour II.
Your vision and hard work to recreate a vessel
from the era long before engines and electronics,
showed so clearly what a remarkable
achievement it truly was for anyone, of any time,
to sail the high seas under square sails.

: *Ron M. Craig*
: *George Opacic*

Many thanks to those who kindly contributed
their reminiscences to the story:

Andrea Brigola	Ralph Eastland
Joe Klausner	Bill Mitchell
Hans Schaer	David Salt
Jeff Berry	Don Hammond
Adam Fortunate Eagle	

CONTENTS

Building A Dream 1
In a Cloud of Sails 22
Adventure can be a Business 26
More Adventure Than Expected 33
Life On Board 43
Making Ready 50
Are We Ready? 66
Like a Hobby-Horse 70
San Francisco 75
Let's Invade Alcatraz 84
It Had To Be 95
The Coast Guard Doesn't Like Us 99
Hard Lessons at San Diego 107
Details 114
Facts About Sailing the Pacific 117
What To Do In Tahiti 125
Paradise Aftermath 138
Rebirth 140
The Queen Was (not) Pleased 151
How Celebrity Works 155
On the Tasman Sea 165
Plastered in Brisbane 172
To Auckland 177
The End 181
Figures 203

Building A Dream

In the 1960s, Canada's west coast drew many people from Europe who wanted to build their dreams. Most dreams consisted of being free of the confines of the crowded civilization of Europe. They wanted to stretch out to build a house, have a family and work in the highly profitable, and dangerous, industries of fishing, mining or forestry.

Those who kept their dreams general filled the forest with axes and saws, sweated in dark, dusty mines, or hauled over-full nets on the thousands of trawlers along the coast.

A few had a burning in their hearts to control the logging and lumber companies, the mines, or the fish processors. These people worked their way as quickly as they could into the wealthy offices of the owners.

Some people dreamed differently. Their dreams did not mesh well with those around them. At times, that kept them on the outside dreaming dark thoughts. A few of the non-meshing dreams jelled into a shape whose fascinating colours and swirls captured the eyes of people who were disillusioned with the standard colour-palette they worked with on a daily basis.

One such different dreamer was Alexander Brigola. A big man, Alex could sell you his grand dreams and you would stand before him nodding until you found yourself handing over thousands of dollars, or the equivalent in goods, for the privilege of being a shareholder in his dream.

In 1965, Alex's dream was to build a three-masted sailing ship which throngs of admiring landlubbers would pay to board at ports around the Mediterranean.

Figure 1 Alex Brigola

Once the vision captured his imagination it became all-consuming. It was pervasive, spreading from Alex's piercing eyes to anyone he focused on.

In an old building by the northwest foot of the Second Narrows Crossing, North Vancouver, British Columbia, he and his fellow dreamers went to work on their impossible project. Joe, Hans, Crazy George and a few others spent long days with Alex, converting the grand vision into plans and practical lengths of Douglas Fir and Sitka Spruce beams and ribs.

As the project attracted serious interest over the next couple years, "shareholders" who did not have time to contribute their labour, such as Ron C. Craig and Paul K. Haggard, took on the roles of negotiating with suppliers, raising money and promoting the project. The group came to rely on Ron to perform miracles in attracting the support of a few major corporate interests and government ministers.

Ron was a man who got things done. He owned the successful and biggest toy supplier distributorship in Western Canada, located next to Carlings Brewery in Vancouver, called West Coast Toy & Hobby. Ron also promoted the Jolly Jumper around the world in 1964. This took him to Japan during the Olympics of that year, and to Germany, England and Egypt, where he visited the pyramids, getting to ride a camel there. He was also in the camper business at that time. His company, called Astronaut Camper Mfg., was located on East Esplanade, a few blocks away from where the ship was being built.

While in North Van on business, Ron had heard about the unusual project from Joseph Poole, who owned the Jolly Jumper factory. They were discussing sales strategies when Joe casually said, "Maybe we should use that wooden ship they're building over at Lynnwood Marina. Once they launch that thing, its picture will be in all the newspapers."

"Ship?"

"Yes, a big wooden ship. We could call the papers, hang a few Jolly Jumpers from the front and bob's your uncle! The best of both worlds! A sailing ship and smiling babies."

Ron was intrigued. He had to drive down to the Marina to see what the fuss was about.

He was directed to a yard behind Lynnwood Marina and the B.C. Fiberglas plant. As Ron walked around the buildings the morning sun was just rising over the Second Narrows bridge. It illuminated a framework of delightfully curved planks, marking the massive hull of a true wooden sailing ship under the canopy gridwork. Ron was transfixed.

Building A Dream

Figure 2 Hull under construction, January 1967

Let us step back, to years before the north shore of Burrard Inlet was settled by the British.

Young James Cook of Yorkshire, Great Britain, was fortunate to be accepted as an apprentice seaman in the service of John Walker. The Walkers owned ships that took coal, primarily, to the insatiable furnaces of London and across the treacherous North Sea. Walker treated his apprentice more than fairly, giving him lodging in his house, and, when not working aboard ship, permitting him the rare privilege of reading all of the impressive library of texts that he had on navigation, shipbuilding and seamanship.

James surprised himself when he found that he had an uncanny ability in mathematics. He also had a prodigious memory for details. When he read a book, he applied its lessons at the earliest opportunity. Another admirable quality that young James had was not wishing to impose himself on others, despite knowing that a task being done by a superior might not be on a path to achieve the desired result. He filed away such incidents until he was to be in charge.

It took a mere five years for James Cook to rise from a teen-age seaman to mate of a ship he had helped build for the Walkers. As mate, he was senior officer of the 600-ton merchant collier (coal-carrier) the Friendship. Every minor peculiarity of the ship offered him information about its health and how to improve it.

Were James Cook to look down onto the new hull in the shadow of the Second Narrows Crossing, he would have cringed quietly.

Foresters and seamen alike know that trees are either hardwood or softwood. The oak structure of a rugged Whitby collier, like those Captain Cook served on, were designed by experienced mariners and fashioned by tradesmen whose life-long work was building the best vessels they could, designed for a particular purpose. Their wide, solidly built hold would take the pounding seas for decades. Used in a narrow-beamed ship that was designed only for *looks*, softwood like Douglas fir or Sitka spruce would appear sufficient but would last only a few years.

These maritime skills had been largely lost over the years. If they were to be found again, someone had to be brave enough to put a wooden hull in the water. Alex Brigola knew he was the man to do that.

Speaking to Ron Craig, Brigola said, "My friend, whose young imagination has not been captured by a picture of a graceful wooden sailing ship on the open sea? This is a project of the heart. It must be built!"

Still staring at the surprising size of the hull that first morning, Ron knew he had to be part of this adventure. "Alex, this is a once in a lifetime opportunity. What can I do to help?"

Knowing that he and the other builders were fully engaged in the details of drafting and construction, "Thank you, Ron. What we need is someone to organize the support, to speak with people in government, to plan for the future of this endeavour. Are you willing to invest your time and money?"

Without hesitation, "I'm on board!"

So, they each set about applying their individual talents to the grand task.

Alex had a well-deserved reputation as one who did not suffer fools easily. When he decided that something needed to be done, then, by God, it would be done! He would get along with Ron very well because they both had been captured by the vision of a cloud of sails bursting through the blue Pacific waves. Nothing would deter them from putting their vision to life in the waters of Burrard Inlet.

Another person who was to make an indelible mark on Alex's ship-to-be at a later date, recalled *his* first sight of a sailing ship. Jeff Berry:

> When I was able to go to school, my very first day was eventful. Mother dropped me off in front of the school, made sure I had my lunch and left with, "Have a good day!"
>
> As I walked with some trepidation to the front door, a group of the older children saw me approach. It was like a young doe walking into the midst of a wolf pack. They surrounded me and started by asking what I had in the bag. The gang leader grabbed my lunch bag and rummaged around in it. "Nothing good in here," he proclaimed.
>
> Then they played with their prey, pushing me from one to the other. I was tripped and about to be kicked when an angelic sight burst from the front door of the school to swoop upon the gang. She was, to my child's mind, an older woman, but thinking back, she must have been no more than eighteen. Her flowing golden locks danced about her shoulders. Her newly hand-made dress fit her like a princess. She told off the ruffians and bent down to gently lift me off the dusty ground.
>
> "Are you hurt? You must be young Jeffrey. Come with me." She led me into her room. It was, as I recall, not well lit. Sitting there while my guardian angel went to the principal's office, I took in the contents of her inner sanctum. On the wall was a calendar, brightly lit by a ray of sunshine. Its picture was of a marvelous sailing vessel, painted with sails full of a strong wind, bursting through foamy white waves. I couldn't take my eyes off it. The painting drew me to it like a magnet. I flipped up the calendar's pages to reveal one glorious painting of a sailing ship after the next. Some ships danced gracefully with porpoises leaping ahead of the ship's bow; there were seagulls wheeling around a cloud

of sails; one showed a gnarled captain leaning into a gale next to a wooden mast… I was hooked.

When I returned home my mother asked if I had learned anything interesting at school. I said, "Yes. I know what I want to be when I grow up!"

"She nodded patiently, 'That's nice, Jeffrey.' She was expecting something like my wanting to be a cowboy or a major-general. When I said, 'I want to be a sailing ship's captain!', she was not pleased.

When her same question was asked weeks later, and she received my same firm answer, mother shook her head. "Jeffrey, there are no sailing ship captains any more. And besides, the men a captain would have to lead are, well, uncouth."

I devoted most of my free time in those early years to prove to mother that, yes, there were sailing ship captains. Over the years I had to agree with her that seamen could be uncouth. But they were also more real and full of raw life than a city packed with clerks.

Alex Brigola had modelled his own dream from a picture, as well. It was of the brigantine, *Albatross*, in Uffa Fox's *Second Book of Boats*. This dream ship, confided Alex, would bring him the praise that he yearned for in his new country. And it was bound to rake in mounds of cash. When pressed for a long term plan, Alex proclaimed that he would "sail it to the Mediterranean to cruise the coast like the tall ships of old".

Figure 3 The Albatross, from http://de.academic.ru/dic.nsf/dewiki/45845

For the non-sailor, a *brigantine* is a *two*-masted ship with the rearward mast sometimes having an upper square sail over an arrangement of triangular sails, usually with one called a spanker (in fig, 3, this is the rearmost sail with an angled boom holding the canvas). The foremast is square-rigged (all square sails).

A *barque*, like most Whitby colliers, has three or more masts with the rear mast, termed the mizzenmast, usually holding a spanker. The triangular sails on the front are called jibs, while a variety of triangular staysails may come off the mizzenmast. The purpose of the many sails is to capture as much wind as one can, under many different conditions. The aerodynamics involved is quite complex. Square-rigged ships are very different from yachts.

Figure 4   The barque Monte Cristo under full sail

And, mariners rarely refer to "tall ships". To a seaman, that is a contrived term, originating in flowery poems by landlubbers.

> Peering up into the canvas draped over the fresh hull at Lynnwood Marina, we may see a ghostly Captain Cook sitting with a hand slapped to his face.

His head will continue to shake as Alex and the hard working shareholders lay timber for the *Monte Cristo*, as Alex named the ship.

Bravely forging ahead with unfamiliar tasks, they made up what they could not discern from pictures. Incomplete and sometimes incorrectly read examples of how to build a wooden ship were translated into spars and ribs that were fashioned to "look right".

Joe Klausner was called on to make hardware whose names and full purpose were not previously part of his life's experience. He did a remarkable job, nonetheless, keeping the project going with his inventiveness and metalworking skill.

> Being from an era when every little part on a ship had been crafted with a particular purpose, technique, material, and form – because sailors' lives depended on it – Captain Cook was not impressed with Alex's design.
>
> "That chain-plate has not the strength to resist a year's worth of gales hauling on its shrouds, and by God if it has no backing-plate the bolts will worry through the timber before you see King George's Island!"

Sailing to King George's Island – Tahiti – was not on Alex's current agenda. There was too much to be done in convincing suppliers to contribute to the grand project, and encouraging the workers to stay all day, converting his drawings into huge lengths of timber that steadily took on the shape of a graceful sea-going vessel.

> The ghost of Captain Cook wished he could move Alex's drawing pencil to his wishes.
>
> "If you place the beams there, the foremast will be too close to the mainmast and her lines will foul on a hard tack. No! You don't use the deck as the basis for her calculations, you use the waterline! My God, man! The hollow entry of the cut-water will not have sufficient buoyancy to lift her bow in heavy seas and the fashion-timbers are nothing but over-large, pretty skirts!"

Without the experience afforded by grizzled mariners, the modern-day builders worked on, being pulled irresistibly by the lure of their dream ship as if it had taken hold of their hearts, causing them to build its own life. Creating the *Monte Cristo* became an all-consuming task.

With mounting debts in the early summer of 1968, Alex pulled back on his dream of taking his ship to Europe. At a meeting of the financial shareholders in the Bayshore Inn, Vancouver, called by a concerned Ron C. Craig, Alex proclaimed his new vision to be a more modest one of sailing the Pacific coast of Canada and the United States, gaining fame and great fortune by inviting the throngs of paying landlubbers on board. Their company would be called the *Monte Cristo Charter Line*.

Ron, Paul and the other financial backers were now seeing this dream ship through different eyes, tinted by red ink.

Figure 5 Under construction

The *Monte Cristo*, however, cared not for the machinations of mortals. She needed to be built.

Joe Klausner and his friend Hans Schaer were the mechanical experts who kept plodding forward with needed hardware. While a picture may show rigging with penciled lines and general attachment points, it was up to these two to determine what actual material, strength and size were needed to make it work.

Figure 6 Shareholder Certificate

Building A Dream

There was a determined cast of characters. Jri Novak was a strapping young deserter from the Czechoslovakian army. If there was a huge beam to lift into place, he was the willing man. Crazy George helped in his own weird way. Ron's son, young Ron Jr., still unsure of his path in life, initially vacillated between the ship and girls. Other "shareholders" at this time included Arnold Brigge, Jamie Wright, Greg Lee, Buddy Whitehead, Doug Starlatt and Gordy Calder.

On either side of the old shed that had given birth to the *Monte Cristo* were smaller sheds where the workers/shareholders could sleep if they wished, and eat meals. Being European, Alex arranged hearty suppers for those who had worked all day. He had started by providing lunch as well. He quickly saw that a substantial lunch served mainly to put his workers to sleep in the afternoon, so that was ended quietly.

Long days of hard work saw the hull taking full shape. It had outgrown its original shed and now was looking like a real ship.

By May 1968, the hull of the *Monte Cristo* was sufficiently complete to do the ultimate reality check. It was time to get it wet. Ron Sr. was able to obtain the donation of about a quarter mile of rail tracks and ties from CN Rail to roll the ship down from the shed to the waters of

Figure 7 Rolling toward the shore, next to the Second Narrows Crossing

Building A Dream

Burrard Inlet. A D-9 Caterpillar tractor would do most of the hauling. Tugs would then tow her to drydock for the finishing work.

Safely hauled from the temporary rail-line into the water by two tugs, the *Monte Cristo* was towed to the east side of the bridge to Ballantyne Pier. Here, she was drydocked so the masts that had been hewn to careful dimensions could be installed with cranes.

An old diesel engine was dropped down into the engine compartment and attached to the propeller. Joe and Hans struggled with the engine's placement and controls.

In mid-May, 1968, the *Monte Cristo* was formally launched with the blessing of a member of cabinet in the provincial government, Phil Gagliardi.

Hundreds of people were disappointed on the first day of the scheduled launch, as the tide was not quite high enough.

On the second day, May 16th, with much grunting from the crew, the *Monte Cristo* slid into the water. From the east side of Burrard Inlet, the ship, sporting her naked masts, was towed to Mosquito Creek near Lions Gate Bridge. There, she would become a proper square-rigged ship.

For the next few months, mariner's terms such as yards, sheets, lines, shrouds and stays would be in common usage by Alex, Joe and Hans as they spent many long nights figuring out how to rig the masts and sails so they stayed firmly aligned in the heaviest of winds. This had all been well established over the past few hundred years, of course. The problem was knowing which questions to ask and where to look for the answers.

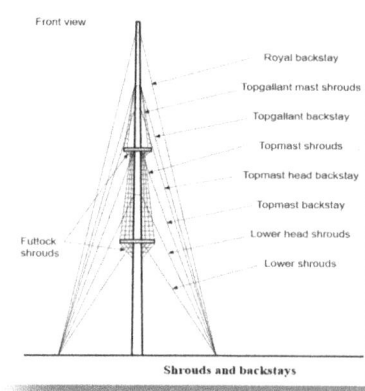

Figure 8 from Rules for Classification and Construction Ship Technology: http://www.gl-

Building A Dream

Had he a voice with which to speak, Captain Cook would have said, "*At the very least, you must consult a new text such as* David Steel's **The Elements and Practice of Rigging, Seamanship, and Naval Tactics, Including Sail Making, Mast Making, and Gunnery**, 1821. *Or* John Cock's **A treatise on mast-making**, 1840."

Ron Craig Jr. was soon promoted to the technical crew. Those other young builders who had been at their tedious work for long months did not easily accept Ron Jr.'s immediate placement into the more interesting work of helping Joe and Hans with the steel fittings and rigging calculations. There was muttered discontent.

Monte Cristo's spirit ignored the melodrama. It demanded of them that they continue laying planks and attaching hardware.

The *Report of Inspection*, by Marine Surveyors of Western Canada, submitted on the Monte Cristo in 1968, included an assessment of the materials and Joe's metalworking, at p. 8:

"The workmanship throughout appears to be of a high standard.

"The trees from which the masts and yards were shaped, reportedly were hand picked, transported to Vancouver following which all masts and yards were hand hewn.

"Iron work on masts including trusses, stirrups, parrals, hound bands, etc. were forged by one of the building crew who doubles as a welder and blacksmith.

Figure 9   Joe Klausner

Building A Dream

"Fuel and fresh water tanks were made by this crew member.

"All deadeyes were turned and iron work fitted, all chain plates were made up by crew members. All rigging was cut, spliced and fitted according to rigging manuals and deadeyes and lanyards are set up in the proper manner."

As with many schemes of the heart rather than of the mind, trouble was brewing in the account books.

It was a standing joke among the people working on the *Monte Cristo* that if Alex needed a box of bolts for the project, he would offer the hardware store owner a share in the vessel. Many people around Vancouver became "shareholders". Finally, it came to a head. Ron Sr., Paul and the other financial shareholders had to go to court to wrest the nearly bankrupt ship project away from the dreamer, Alex.

Figure 10 Painting the hull

On an early winter afternoon in 1968, Ron Jr. was told to meet his father during one of Ron Sr.'s hurried business trips through Vancouver. They met at a quiet restaurant in North Vancouver near the ship. While chilly, they only needed light coats. Ron Jr.

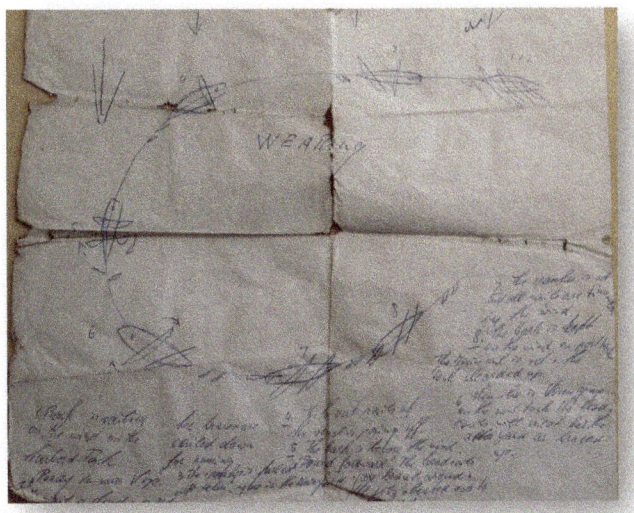

Figure 11 Brigola's notes on sailing

hung his coat on the back of his chair. Ron Sr. was in a distracted mood and kept his coat on.

As soon as the server gave them their coffees, Sr. pulled out a sheaf of papers from inside his coat, making room for them on the table.

"Son, I need to cash out the six apartments that I placed in your name. Sign here."

"Huh?" Young Ron remembered something about having official ownership of the small apartments. It was a method of deferring taxes, he'd been told.

Handing his son a pen, Sr. was upset, "I have to force Alex out. The Charter Line has been slapped with an excise tax of $50,000!"

"What? What in the world is that for? We don't…" Ron Jr. had no idea there could be such a thing as a tax on all their essentially free, hard work, on a dream project like the *Monte Cristo*.

Ron Sr. had dealt with government demands before. "Whatever they want to tax, they can. Nothing to do but pay it now and fight it later.

Alex wants to run the ship someplace to get away from the tax, but you can't do that. He's going bonkers and if we don't force him out, the rest of us are going to lose our shirts.

"Listen, the apartments can bring in $35,000 each, and I can sell the limo business to the two drivers who've been with me from the start. I'm selling Astronaut Camper Mfg. to Jim. That cash and a Corvette from my dealership in Alberta should be enough to save the project from Alex's reckless dreaming. We pay the government and pay him off and get back to business."

Ron Jr. kept a journal for a few months, reflecting that period.

From Ron Jr.'s diary, front page, starting in January, 1969:

Monte Cristo, W.B., Vancouver, BC

Type – Square Rigged Wind Barque

Weight 94 tons, R.T. 91

Length Stern to Tip 94'

Length Stern to Tip of Jib Boom 131'

Masts 80' – 85'

Waterline Length 71'

February 24th, 1969: *Worked on boat.*

Tuesday 25th: *On Monte Cristo.*

Wednesday 26th: *Lost drivers licence today. I'll get it back when I get insurance.*

Friday 28th: *Worked at ship all day. Got paid 58$. Got drunk. Donna and I at 1 month now.*

Saturday 1st March: *Moved out of old apt. On ship full time now.*

Building A Dream

Sunday 2nd March: *Finished moving out of my apt. Tim and I caught a cab to the Boat. Judy & Sue came over. Judy & Sue went and got my girlfriend Donna. Tim is going to ask Dad for a job on the Boat tonight. He asked and got the job. Got Tim's clothes from Richmond.*

Monday 3rd: *Tim and I got up at 10:00. Ate and we started work. Dad had to go to court over Boat business. Tim likes working on the Boat. We started an exercise kick tonight which we hope to keep up. We are listening to records and then we are going to hit the sack. Glad Tim moved out of Stew's. He's more like a brother than a friend. Tim's talking to Judy.*

Ron Jr. and the other workers were as hooked by the project as any young man could be. For some, the vision hooked them immediately. Others took a month, with the *Monte Cristo* gradually replacing different interests.

Captain Cook smiled at the enthusiastic young workers. *"It is ever the way. Were it not for the clouded young minds and their willing backs, our exploration of distant lands would have extended little beyond a day's walk from mother's milk.*

Things came to a head on a late spring morning, 1969. The *Monte Cristo* was docked at Mosquito Creek for a last bit of work prior to setting off. The crew had finished with her rigging and sail adjustments. Her cabins were prepared with a wide range of exotic woods.

Figure 12 The ship drew visitors

Building A Dream

Enthusiasm for the imminent setting of sails was clouded by darker mumblings in the cabin. It became common knowledge that the court case brought by Ron Sr. and the other financial shareholders, resulting from the tax bill, was going to be decided against Alex.

Figure 13   Port & starboard sides of the main cabin

Distraught, seeing that his dream was to be wrenched from him at this time of its realization, Alex fumed silently in his bunk on board. Alex feverishly made a plan. That evening he resolved to see if any of the crew of the *Monte Cristo* were with him. At this point, Alex could no longer think clearly. The world was constricting against him.

He waited until the crew had all returned from visiting their favourite pubs in North Van. As they were gathering in the newly furnished main cabin for their usual card game and chat, Alex joined them. There was tension in the air as he sat at one of the benches.

Alex spoke over the forced chatter with terse tones. "Men, you know that there will be changes around here."

Sullen nods, not wanting to provoke Alex's quick temper. At least one of the workers – soon-to-be-seamen – was embarrassed. "Listen, skipper. It ain't right what they're doing to you…"

Alex waved it off. "They won fair and square. I don't have the money to carry on and they do. So that's it, then."

He lifted a sly eye to see who might still be on his side. Every head stayed down or nodded to his last comment.

He thought, *Well alright then. I'm on my own.*

Keeping his tension in check as well as he could, "Nothing left to do about it, men. Anyways, we'll have a jolly good time with me as the skipper, sailing down to Seattle! Won't we?"

A few reluctant nods.

"Alright, then. Before we sail this fine ship out past English Bay, they've authorized me to take you all to a damn good breakfast tomorrow. I want everyone of you to be at the Bayshore before seven. So get a good night's sleep and I'll see you there. Might be late – I have a quick meeting with the, ah, new owners – so start without me."

The prospect of a breakfast over in Vancouver, across Burrard Inlet, livened up their spirits. They politely wished Alex a good night and wrapped up their game quickly.

Next morning, after the last of the crew left for Vancouver, Alex got to work. He checked the fuel on board, again. He hauled in the mooring lines himself, hopped below to quickly start the diesel, and climbed back up to loose the last mooring line. One of the workers at the marina gave a surprised wave as Alex and his ship left.

Figure 14 Figurehead, carved by Brigola

Unfortunately, the *Monte Cristo* was not of a type that could be sailed by a crew of fewer than five or six men for a day trip. Fifteen to twenty would be needed for an ocean voyage. Within minutes Alex was overwhelmed. Manhandling her in the calm waters of Burrard Inlet was hard enough. He was barely able to motor her under the Lions Gate Bridge when the open wind of English Bay hit the tall masts. Even with her sails furled, the wind drove her bow toward shore. To make things fully impossible, the tide was coming in. Without help, the little diesel was no match for both implacable forces of nature. And Alex simply couldn't handle the tiller and engine himself. Seeing that the shore was coming irresistibly closer, with a huge struggle he managed to drop the smaller midships anchor. As soon as he could, he scrambled down to the old wireless that had just been installed to send out a distress call to the Harbour Master.

Fortunately, a tug was in the vicinity. It was dispatched in time to toss the *Monte Cristo* a line and be towed ignominiously back to Mosquito Creek.

Alex was ordered to report immediately on docking to the Harbour Master.

Saying that he had been injured, he agreed to report when he was released from hospital. Alex wasn't seen again in the Vancouver area. Word was that he hopped a train back to Quebec and from there left on a ship to Europe.

The word was wrong. Alex and his family moved quietly to Lions Bay to set up a new life.

He kept dreaming. The house he built there was a prominent, well-remarked feature on the wooded slope over Howe Sound for many years. As an accomplished carver, Alex's daughter recalled that he mentored carvers who recreated totem poles in Stanley Park.

Eventually, a great ship's hull began to take shape on the shore next to Britannia Mine. Trying once more, Alex pushed past the reality that it would have taken a million real dollars to complete that dream.

With the everyday facts of life pressing on the dream, the years finally captured the hull into a death grip. Like a great beached whale, that hull dissolved into the sand.

Figure 15   Another ship?

In a Cloud of Sails

The sight of a sailing ship's broad white sails captures many a heart. They speak of journeys to far lands, where adventure will challenge the stuff of which you are made.

There will be sailors with you who become closer than brothers, and there will be people who stand obstinately in the way of your dream. Fights may occur over matters large and small.

Figure 16   Monte Cristo / Endeavour II

For some, the challenge lies in the technical capability of shepherding a large, complex wooden and canvas vessel along the fickle waterways of the vast Pacific.

A few see profit in the hazy cloud of sails.

If we gaze up into the canvas we might see the images of past vessels. Were they any different from today's sailing ships? Before steam, the commerce of the world ran on the decks of wooden square-riggers.

In a Cloud of Sails

Fast-forward, to the mid-1900s, several similar ships sailed the seas, but their purpose was generally for entertainment.

More than is recognized by most historians, England's early success on the seas relied on the rugged design of the vessels that Captain Cook first sailed on as a lad. The *Whitby collier* was not the fastest of designs. But they weathered the worst of storms and kept sailing. As the famous Captain's spirit could be heard in the rigging, saying,

> *If only the Monte Cristo had actually followed the lines of a collier, she would have stood a chance.*

The quest for profit in the heady period of world exploration of the mid-1700s saw these sturdy English vessels compete with Dutch, Portuguese and Spanish merchant ships, all with their individual designs. They often found themselves in the same bays on the opposite side of the world and often at cross purposes.

> ***Cook's Journals - First Voyage** - July 7th, 1771, p. 211:*
>
> *Winds NNE & NW. Courses N 50° E. Distance sailed in miles 49...*
>
> *Gentle breezes & clear weather...*
>
> *At 9 am spoke to a Brig from Liverpool bound to Porto and some time after another from London bound to the Grenades, she had been three days from Scilly...*
>
> *We learnt from this vessel that no accounts had been received in England from us and that wagers were held that we were lost, it seems highly improbable that the letters sent by the Dutch ships from Batavia should not be come to hand, as it is now five months since these ships sailed from the Cape of Good Hope.*

Not all ship's captains played nice. Rivalries between ships were played out on a global scale.

And why would a Yorkshire businessman like John Walker of Whitby want to sink his family's hard-earned money into a small fleet of sailing ships when easy fortunes were being made on shore? Captains of England's Industrial Age built private factories that were designed to secure and exploit trade secrets, such as how to weave cotton into cloth inexpensively, in ever greater quantities. New inventions, like automated looms and steam-powered water pumps for ever deeper coal mines were creating a new wealthy class.

One might ask, at that time in England, why use one's new fortune just to have a wooden ship built? The historically accurate version is given as a rational process.

> ***Cook's Journals – Introduction***, *edited by Philip Edwards, p. 9:*
>
> *However important these voyages were for geographical knowledge and the advancement of science... all these expeditions by the competing European powers of Spain, France and Britain were undertaken for the control of new territory for commercial exploitation and strategic use.*

In fact, there was treasure to be found in the far lands. The new class of enterprising business people rubbed their hands at the prospect of spices, cotton, furs and gold that seemed to lie around for the picking. If they were there first.

Then again, what brought a lad from a small farming village in Yorkshire to the sea, and onto a wooden vessel hauling dusty coal up and down the eastern coast of England and across the dangerous waters of the North Sea? Would you take that highly risky career move?

As explained by a writer who looked into the soul of young James Cook, the answer is a less rational decision than a businessman would make.

> ***Great Sailor***, *by John W. Vandercook, pp 14-15:*
>
> *All tastes are strange to those who do not share them. None, to a convinced landsman, is harder to understand than a love for the sailor's calling... Bad weather – bad, foul and intolerable – is the rule. Winds are cruel and currents tricky... The cave-dark quarters below deck where the crew swung their hammocks were almost perpetually wet. Food, though not outright rotten as so often in the Navy and on all long voyages, was monotonous, cheap, and abominably cooked.*

The profession that James Cook had chosen did offer one supreme reward. In that reward lies the clue to the repeated mystery. The basic fact of survival was daily bought at the price of skill. If you learned quickly enough the seaman's arts, you lived. If you did not, or if you grew clumsy or forgetful, you died.

That sharp, private joy which comes from the body's aptness, the hands' and the mind's cleverness gaining quiet, recurring victories against the heavy forces of God and earth and the sea, is one of the great intangibles, one of the strongest motivations of the human spirit... The experience of life earned and earned again by wits and courage cannot be bought or borrowed. It can scarcely be communicated.

Once learned, some find it is all they really care for.

Figure 17   Capt. James Cook - statue in Victoria's Inner Harbour, British Columbia

Adventure can be a Business

The *Monte Cristo Charter Line Ltd.* was a company. All it needed was a ship in the water and a good skipper to sail her.

Ron C. Craig was the right Owner to move the project ahead. He would find a gnarly old skipper to take the ship along the coast to make money at the many maritime events.

Figure 18 1970 – Ron C. Craig in Australia, before a painting of Capt. James Cook

Ron had a good business sense, from the marketing side, with successful businesses in several cities. Ron's strength was in his network of important people in government and in cities across Canada as well as in the USA.

Ron would wryly admit that he did not always make the best choices. He had been selling a novelty item for cars such as the newly popular Volkswagen Beetle. His "Continental" kit was a hit for those who liked to attach what looked like the grill of a limousine to their little putt-putt. That success brought the offer of a Volkswagen dealership in Alberta. Ron declined, saying that the Bug was just a short-run fad.

Other than that one miss, Ron generally had a good sense for what the public wanted. He was certain that the *Monte Cristo Charter Line* would be a hit with companies that wanted to treat their management and staff with a special event on the high seas. Everybody was enthralled with sailing ships, weren't they?

Ron was well thought of by all who knew him. Later in life, at his place in Palm Springs, the regulars called him *Skipper*. Ron Jr., while not as committed to the *Monte Cristo* as Ron Sr., had been suitably impressed when he found his father's address book once. It contained Marlon Brando's personal phone numbers, along with those of Cher's mother, and that of the Prime Minister of New Zealand.

Ron Sr. had no qualms about picking up the phone to speak with any

Figure 19 Docked at Mosquito Creek (see it?)

mover or shaker he felt could help him achieve his goals.

The *Monte Cristo* needed more than an Owner on shore. She needed a Skipper with experience in sailing square-riggers. The man that fit the bill seemed to be a local character by the name of Captain Gilchrist.

Capt. Tom Gilchrist was taken on after Alex Brigola tried to make off with the *Monte Cristo*. The old sea-dog had an impressive résumé, having sailed the western coast of Canada for years, on ships that he stated included large sailing ships. Currently, and more easily authenticated, Gilchrist had been a writer for radio and television shows including the popular "Tidewater Tramp" on the CBC.

As Captain Tom (as Ron Sr. called him) took the *Monte Cristo* on sea trials in Burrard Inlet and English Bay, Ron made long term plans for his company of adventurers. The British Columbia government was going to participate at a major trade exhibit in Osaka, Japan: Expo '70. Ron established the contacts and first broached the possibility of a cross-Pacific voyage with Captain Gilchrist, then having the vessel as a feature at Expo '70.

Meanwhile, the crew had to be paid, so Ron

Figure 20 Crew Aloft

Adventure can be a Business

arranged for his ship to be the major draw at upcoming local marine events like the Kitsilano Yacht Club's *Sail Past*, the Vancouver *Sea Festival*, and summer festivals in Victoria, Nanaimo and Powell River.

The 1969 sailing season started off well for the *Monte Cristo* in April. Dale Lawrence wrote glowingly of the perfect combination of weather and yachts:

> "It's not likely anyone who took part in the *Lower Mainland's Opening Weekend* will ever forget the spectacle on English Bay as hundreds of boats turned out in sparkling sunshine to make it the greatest opening bash of all time… Kitsilano YC and Hollyburn Sailing Club climaxed the big weekend by blanketing the bay with their sailing fleets on Sunday afternoon. The scene was dominated by the three-masted barque *Monte Cristo*, which anchored off Kitsilano and served as the flagship."

Promotion of the ship was easy. Arranging for the *Monte Cristo* to be featured at marine events was merely a matter of sending the brochure to organizers. Making money at the appearances was a hard slog. It took Ron Sr.'s dedicated efforts to prepare signage, have the crew trained to deal with visitors, and collect a meagre entrance fee at each dockside.

Figure 21 Monte Cristo brochure

Adventure can be a Business

Broadening the opportunities, Ron Sr. obtained a business license for his charter company in the State of Washington, with plans to take the USA west coast by storm.

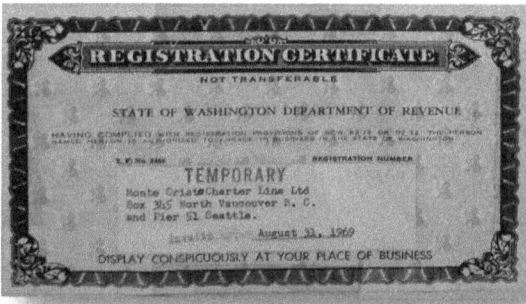

Figure 22 Monte Cristo Charter Line USA registration

Joe and Hans had given their notice to Ron Sr. as the construction and rigging had been completed. They had agreed to be around the project for another few weeks but were in demand for their engineering skills in the real world. Part of his remaining tasks was replying to queries from potential crew, so Hans had replied to a letter that was sent from Hong Kong by a young fellow who sorely

Figure 23 Berth at Bayshore Inn, Vancouver

Adventure can be a Business

wanted to sail on a square-rigger. That man's name was Jeff Berry. He was to join the crew as soon as he could arrange passage.

Meanwhile, the less-than-exciting tasks of sailing to one town after another, swabbing the ship down, and dealing with the same excited questions from crowds of youngsters was wearing on some of the young crew. There was turnover, until a number of prairie farmers came aboard.

With prospects of actually sailing onto the open Pacific, the dozen or more regular workers/seamen began getting stars in their eyes. In the manner of olden times, these new crewmen those drawn to the dream of sailing on the *Monte Cristo* were eager young lads who came from the farms of Saskatchewan looking for adventure.

Shortly it would be time to exchange their excited discussions about sailing off to distant lands, with having their destiny entirely in each other's hands on the great heaving Ocean.

Figure 24 Welcomed at the Bayshore Inn, Vancouver

The ship's dock was a hive of focused activity aloft and below decks.

Bill Mitchell was a crew member while the ship was still safely sailing the British Columbia and Washington inner coasts. He had a lot of fond memories:

Adventure can be a Business

I don't like heights so I remember being vertically challenged the first few times I climbed the mast to either look out from the "crow's nest" or, more gut wrenching, climbing out onto the yardarm to furl or unfurl a sail. It was especially challenging when we were in rolling seas and the mast was swaying from side to side. As you might remember we didn't have any safety equipment as we climbed the rigging and out onto the yardarms standing on a wire as we leaned over to hold onto the sails.

More Adventure Than Expected

In the white shrouds of the *Monte Cristo*, Captain Cook's long shadow fumed.

> *This ship has been built with no purpose! Having no purpose, it is an abomination! Is she to traipse about the shore, in protected shoals, playing nursemaid to landsmen, or is she to sail the far seas, over which I have navigated with crews of brave mariners?*
>
> *"In three expeditions aboard ships tried and true, I can modestly say that I have made no very great discoveries, yet I have explored more of the Great South Sea than all that have gone before me!"*
>
> *With this I give fair warning to the Monte Cristo. Beware! This ship without a purpose, constructed on a whim, crewed by landsmen with no training, the sea shall rise up to smite you!*

Captain Gilchrist was very pleased to have found such a prestigious posting as Skipper of an actual square-rigger. To celebrate on the first evening of his appointment, he had treated himself to a few drinks in Vancouver. Actually, he needed no excuse to partake of a few drinks. With his captain's hat jauntily perched over his white hair, Gilchrist was a familiar figure striding along the sidewalk to his regular drinking establishment. On entering the still empty pub, he was greeted warmly by the bartender.

"Captain Tom! We missed you yesterday. Were you at the television studio?"

"My usual, Rick. Is the new waitress…"

"Emily?"

"Is Emily working tonight?" His lecherous expression could not be mistaken.

Rick received a cut of whatever proceeds his girls made, so he was genuinely disappointed to say, "Sorry, Captain. Emily didn't show up since you saw her last… What happened between…"

Gruffly, "Nothing. Forget about her. Give me a double for now."

Rick had poured an almost double whiskey. He came around the bar with the drink. "Here. I can sit with you for a few minutes." They took a table in front of the bar.

Gilchrist cupped the glass reverently for a bit then downed a satisfying quantity. Rick nodded. "My best whiskey. For my best captain and favourite movie star. So, did you take that job?"

With a broad smile, Gilchrist appreciated his audience. "Yes, I decided to accept the position. I am in the middle of writing a new novel – a murder mystery on the high seas – so I felt it would be…" he easily downed the remainder of the glass, pushing it toward Rick for a refill, "so I want to use this as research." He allowed a twinkle in his eye.

Smiling, Rick got up, taking the glass behind the bar for another almost double.

A few more glasses and Gilchrist was immune to the slings of the world.

With a slur now on his tongue, Gilchrist propounded, "So I told him, this is what I want and nobody else in the world can sail her for you!" His fist pounded the table, jiggling his glass.

Encouraging the old man, as much for the entertainment as for the fact that the pub contained only one young couple in the corner sipping on a single glass of wine between them, Rick prodded. "So you've been captain on a tall ship before?"

The whiskeys were finally slowing Gilchrist down. "Well. Sort of." He leaned closer to Rick across the table. "Just a ketch. And I was on a schooner too. But it's all the same, isn't it? It's wind pushing canvas…" He waved his arms to create the wind. Arms still up, thinking about it, he added, "Have to read about square sails. They're another kettle of fish…"

Picture Captain Cook in a dark corner giving himself a face-slap.

A week after signing on, the new Skipper had decided to take the freshly-rigged ship on trials out past English Bay. He announced his intention to the crew the afternoon before.

With a young crew, most of whom had never even sailed a small yacht, Gilchrist was anxious to prove his own seamanship.

On the night before their sea trials, Ron Jr. had joined the other crew members in the main cabin.

Figure 25 "Brothers Fore"

Having already taken the *Monte Cristo* out for brief runs in Burrard Inlet – "motoring" is the term used when running with sails furled – the crew was beginning to get into the sailing ship mentality. They especially enjoyed the way young ladies in the pubs swooned over them. To encourage their recognition, most of the crew bought and wore what they felt were sailor's shirts and pants.

More Adventure Than Expected

As usual, of an evening in the main cabin, a card game was begun. Ron Jr. brought out some bottles of beer from the cooler.

"Here you go, fellas. Let's drink to a fine day of sailing tomorrow!"

Ron's friend, Tim, looked more nervous than usual. He downed half a bottle with his first swig.

Trying to calm him, Ron asked how he and Judy were getting along.

"Oh, alright, I guess. She says she can't understand why I spend all day working on the ship and then spend most nights sleeping aboard. Sometimes I wonder…"

Ron sympathized. "Yeah, Donna says the same thing. Women! They just don't get it, do they? You know, when I use Joe's crab net, like the catch for tonight's supper – fresh crab – you can't beat that! And…"

Figure 26 Ron Sr. aloft

He stared deeply into his beer, a grin forming. "You know how we have fun by racing up the rat lines and climbing to the top of the main mast and then wrapping our legs around the royal and holding on as the ship sways, sipping a beer up there and enjoying the view while…"

Then he remembered Tim's fear of heights.

More Adventure Than Expected

He glanced at his friend. Quietly, "Are you going to be alright tomorrow? You know you're going to have to climb up past the main yard. We all have to pull our weight on the sea…"

Tim turned his back and sucked down the rest of his beer.

The next morning broke with a red tinge on the southern horizon.

Captain Gilchrist came aboard early. Ready, he was, to take on his next challenge! Reaching back to the days when he actually skippered a ship (metal-hulled trawler, though it had been) he greeted the crew with gusto as they started rolling out on deck.

"Ahoy there lads! I hope you learned something while building this fine ship!" He looked at each of the crew with sincere hope.

"Young Ron! I'm going to appoint you Mate. That means you are my right hand."

Ron was caught by surprise. He turned to Crazy George, next to him by the mainmast, and shrugged sheepishly. What he received in return was a dagger stare. Others muttered a variety of salty terms. Even a cousin of Ron, a skilled carpenter by the name of Earl who had been working on the ship for a year, joined in the discontented scowls.

Pushing past the less-than-joyous reaction, Gilchrist announced, "We are finally going to put this ship to the test! I have planned a series of sea trials that will show us how she handles. The light westerly on English Bay is forecast to change to a brisk sou'westerly for us out in the Strait, some time this morning. We will motor past Lions Gate Bridge then raise sails and make for the Strait of Georgia…"

He explained the duties of each of the dozen crew members, as well as he could remember them from his past few days of reading.

The crew's sour mood couldn't be dulled by the disconnected instructions that Gilchrist was giving. Jeff Berry, having just joined the crew, whispered explanations and corrections to the group around him. At the first opportunity, they started dispersing across the deck. On the way by, Earl brushed roughly against Ron. A shove back followed, and they were at it in close quarters on the aft deck.

Gilchrist was too surprised to react at first, then started shrilling at them. "Stop that! STOP I SAY!"

The others started to circle around the combatants, encouraging the fight, but Gilchrist pushed through. "Enough! I will have none of that with my crew! If you want to be sailors you will learn to work together!"

The fight broke up, with Gilchrist shoving everybody away. Earl scampered up the mainmast as high as he could. Others busied themselves around the deck or on a yard. Young Ron stood near the wheel breathing hard. His friend Tim, who had been mopping the foredeck during the excitement, shuffled back to offer a few consoling words. "You alright, Ron? What was that about?"

Shaking his head sadly, Gilchrist gave orders to loose the moorings and start the old diesel. The young farmer who said he knew how to work diesel engines went below to coax it awake.

They made way from Mosquito Creek. As planned, the *Monte Cristo* kept her sails furled under the Lions Gate Bridge and until the middle of English Bay. At the skipper's command, the engine was lit off (stopped). Ron relayed the skipper's orders to set sails. The crew who weren't already on a yard scampered aloft, clearing the deck of all but the skipper, Tim, and mate, Ron Jr.

Gilchrist, wanting to impress what he felt would be a huge audience ashore, ordered all sails. He started at the wheel then called Tim over to be helmsman.

With all 8500 square feet of sail set, she was, indeed, a magnificent sight. The light wind caught the canvas as the sails were put to the wind, pushing the wooden ship at a good clip. Gilchrist ordered a tack to starboard, intending to pass Point Atkinson. Then, in the manner of a yacht, he intended to tack aggressively across to Nanaimo.

More Adventure Than Expected

The darkening visage of Captain Cook in the high mainmast royal sail shook with silent anger at Gilchrist's lack of seamanship.

"A square-rigged ship is not some cobble with a maiden's skirt flapping in the breeze! My God, man!"

Waves were a modest three to four feet. Even then, one of the design factors began to show itself. The *Monte Cristo* plunged into each wave then bounced back up – to "hobby-horse" deeply. Neither the skipper nor crew had the experience to know if this was normal. With the aggressive sails aloft driving the light bow into the waves, Tim had to cling onto the wheel tightly, becoming decidedly pale of face.

The narrow-beamed ship with too much sail was quick, but another design flaw appeared – the small rudder had marginal effect. More to the point, the crew had not received the detailed training that a seasoned skipper would have put them through before leaving a safe harbour.

The crew fumbled with their orders, the press of sail overwhelming them. Canvas flapped and yards swung perilously close to fouling against stays on the next mast.

When the skipper ordered "Ready about!" most of the crew returned blank stares from aloft.

They finally understood when a couple of the actual sailors aloft translated what to do.

Jeff Berry had been in the US Navy and had also sailed under canvas. To be ready for square-riggers, he had done extensive reading, so he passed on instructions and random bits of knowledge to others near him. Jeff was a quick learner, as were many on board.

"When you can, stand to windward against a yard so you won't get blown away!" "*Flatten the jib* means to draw down the jib sail so that it is flatter and does have as much draw – it is not carying as much air." And so it went, all hands very busy, literally learning the ropes.

In the US Navy, Jeff had served under too many officers who were full of themselves. He had tempered that knowledge with a strict obedience to command protocol – one did not disparage the skipper. Like Captain Cook, he kept critical thoughts to himself. *Just make it right anyway*, he thought to himself.

> High in a luffing royal sail, Captain Cook's visage could be seen alternately shaking his head sadly, and, nodding at the advice being given individually by Jeff and one of the others.

Almost an hour past Point Atkinson, Gilchrist failed to notice the white caps approaching from the southwest. The storm was upon them in minutes and at that point the *Monte Cristo* was broadside to it. Before he knew what to do, the *Monte Cristo*, horrifyingly, keeled over, the starboard gunnels awash and the sudden gale tossing the terrified crew about in their precarious perches aloft.

Completely at a loss, Gilchrist squealed out, "Shiver the square sails!" Whatever that meant. He agitated the air with flying arms and yelled out what instructions he thought were correct for a schooner in similar distress. This happened to be exactly the wrong thing to do for a square-rigger.

"Hard aport! Tim! Ron! Tell them to haul the lines to put her bow-on!"

Fortunately, the crew aloft couldn't respond, even if they heard the skipper's shrill orders, as they were holding on for dear life.

The skipper was saying, in his high-pitched voice, to bring the bow of the ship into the wind. As it was, the ship quickly found herself "in irons", meaning that she had been slowed to a stall in the water, her ineffective rudder was flapping the surface, and the deck was sitting at a 40-degree slope.

Jeff angrily waved off any move to bring her bow-on to the wind. He yelled instructions to those who could hear him.

On the dangerously sloping deck, young Ron saw the waved instructions from Jeff. He and two others who were now on deck managed to fight their way to the spanker sheets, casting them off. Capt. Gilchrist became apoplectic yelling at them to stop. Ron Jr.

carried on, following Jeff's instructions. The boom swung out over the rail, dipping into the water on the lee side. Next, he and the other two brailed in the spanker. Almost immediately this lessened the pressure aft of the ship's pivot point.

Those aloft with enough sense had listened to Jeff and ignored Gilchrist's frantic high-pitched screams. Jeff directed them to cast off the royal halliards and clew them up. Once they managed to do the same to the topgallants, the *Monte Cristo* was able to stagger downwind and start to recover.

If they had quartered the wind from the bow much longer the masts would likely have failed. Completely unlike a schooner, a square-rigged ship is *not* built to take heavy winds head-on.

Ron Jr. and the few crew on deck struggled until the ship was in control. They pulled her back from a cold, humiliating grave in Georgia Strait.

Ron remembered the day plainly:

> When the storm broke it hit us without warning. Everyone was panicking and did what we could for a few minutes then went into the galley to gain some composure, even as the ship was rolling violently. It was very exciting – everything was bouncing around – organized confusion – propane tanks smashing into things and those of us below decks wide-eyed and nobody knew what to do. I remember the freight-train noise from the wind, ominous creaking from the ship coming from all sides and with her keeled over. Anyways, while in there we looked at each other and I said, if this is it and we're going to die, let's not do it without trying, so out we went again and climbed up. I went and others fell in to play and got the ship in order until we were hauled in to Nanaimo.

A harrowing start, and not even on the high seas, yet. It came as a cold slap of reality to the crew who suddenly realized that safely handling a square-rigged ship was vastly different than they had imagined.

Once they successfully returned to Vancouver, Tim left the ship.

*Figure 27   Gale on Georgia Strait,
Nanaimo Free Press*

Life On Board

A wooden sailing ship is a thing alive. Masts settle into their footings, the stays and lines are cinched ever tighter, sailcloth droops, seams at the garboard streak (the first range of planks laid next to the keel) open and need attention. With her builders having no real mariner's experience, the ship speaks in creaks. A well-built wooden ship doesn't actually creak in normal seas.

This ship had been built without the benefit of the life-long skills of a ship-builder or a sea-farer. The *Monte Cristo* was certainly not as solid as a Whitby collier. An aeronautical term can be applied: she was a collection of ship parts sailing in close formation.

Each pounding wave sent shudders, as the 20th century ship groaned across the narrow width of her

Figure 28 Ron Jr. at the helm, in front of Capt. Gilchrist, on English Bay, Vancouver

timbers and beams. It stretched her rigging and squeezed her deck boards so that she became a noisy creature with a personality of her own. Not knowing any better, the crew believed this to be normal.

Despite these underlying issues, the *Monte Cristo* looked impressive! Even motoring across the calm Burrard Inlet, her three wooden masts festooned with her many yards, she commanded attention. The ship did represent a long and gallant tradition. During weekend regattas on English Bay, with a cautious few sails pulling her through the water, mere yachts looked inadequate.

The fact remained, however, that her original builders had made mistakes that were to be discovered as she sailed further away. She was entirely dependent on the ingenuity and persistence of those people scampering along the lines to keep her out of trouble.

Figure 29 Ron Jr. - Rope work

As happens between men and their technology, the crew grew attached to their ship as a trusted partner, together bravely facing the terrible sea and fickle wind. Each little victory over a salty death was celebrated in the evening by the young men. This intimate relationship between ship and her crew had been accepted as obvious in previous centuries when so many plied the oceans hauling cargo around the world. In modern days, that relationship

Life On Board

sneaks up on a young sailor.

Young James Cook, at the same age as most of this crew, had already been a seasoned Master of a Whitby collier.

> His wispy visage, head shaking slowly, might be glimpsed in a high sail of the *Monte Cristo*, marveling at the spotty work ethic of these 20th century seamen. And yet, he felt a pride that the honourable seafaring tradition may continue.

The *Monte Cristo* had been returned to Mosquito Creek for re-fitting after their adventure on the Strait of Georgia.

One of the problems that contributed to the near disaster was laid at the feet of the way she had been rigged. Rigging was a complicated task that very few mariners in this era knew enough about. A square-rigger has a most intricate arrangement of stays and lines needed to maintain the integrity of the masts and to orient each sail with wind under every possible weather condition. Getting that done correctly while in Burrard Inlet was of critical importance, as it would not be possible to pull over to the side of a sea-lane during a gale for a bit of work.

Ron Jr. recalled that time fondly:

> While we were docked with the ship and they were working to prep it seaworthy, Joe had a crab net that we used to throw over the side of the ship on the North Van side and catch fresh crab, which we ate for dinner on many occasions. The inlet was not as polluted then, I guess? At least we never got sick from it – lol!

> When we moved to the Bayshore Inn dock, eating on board the ship was a real treat as we would all take turns in the galley cooking eggs, lots of hash browns and canned bacon for breakfast. This became a tradition, carried on to all of the ports that we sailed to around the BC coast and down to Seattle and Olympia. As young crewmen it was also a thrill at each port, no matter it be Nanaimo or Seattle – we were treated like celebrities! People would ask us for our autographs, pictures and what duties we had on board the ship.

Life On Board

And I have to tell you the young girls would flock to the ship to see the young crew. Some of the maritime fairs that were on in these different ports that we toured allowed us to really strut our stuff, as we wore our striped uniforms and gear. A lot of times we had parties on board with the young ladies and even some of the mothers would come on board later in the night as well.

I remember as a crew member giving guided tours of the ship to the young kids, and telling them stories like I was an old pirate, about the ship and the gold coins under the main mast for luck. Stories about when they would keel haul the bad crew, etc. We even added in the walking on the plank bit too. It was a lot of fun, as you could see the young kids eyes just wide open with these stories they would hear.

Of course we gave real information to the adults as

Figure 30 Starboard view

well and demonstrated the workings of the ship, and our knot work, and the use of the belaying pins as clubs in case of a battle with another rogue ship crew. Lots of hours working swabbing the decks and oiling the many different types of wood that the ship was made of.

Swabbing, by the way, was not only to clean off the gull deposits. There is a mariner's saying: "If the deck dries, it dies." The wood above the water can dry out so much that it will warp and begin to dry-rot. This is one of the thousands of lessons that had to be learned by the young crew.

Figure 31   Early crew – 1969 – with Ron Craig Sr. at the wheel

Fun, frolic and danger, as Ron Jr. remembered it:

> One time I was racing up to the top and I slipped and missed one of the rungs of the rat line and slipped back down cutting the

Life On Board

inside part of my arm leaving a long scar which I have today. I managed to keep ahold of one of the cables on the way down to the upper topsail. I fell only a couple of feet but it was up so high that my heart was beating double-time!

Figure 32   Vancouver Archives – "CVA 447-7004.2 - Sailing Ship Montecristo"

Another favorite of the crew and myself was climbing into the jib netting under the dolphin striker and going up and down, in and out of the water as the ship sailed along. The nights were beautiful as well, even though we were up and down the BC coast and gulf. With the stars out it was an awesome sight and especially when you lay flat on the deck looking at those stars with the ship rocking back and forth and the rigging moving as well, along with creaking of the ship, the waves splashing off of the sides and the wind in the sails that would be flopping away.

Where else would a lad want to be?

Figure 33   Becoming seamen

Making Ready

Once it became known that a real sailing ship was touring the BC coast, all the marine events from Powell River to Seattle wanted the *Monte Cristo* as an attraction.

It also attracted crew members. This is from Ralph Eastman:

> …in May of 1969 I noticed that there was a large sailboat with square sails visiting Campbell River. Of course being a curious person I had to check it out. The crew took me for a tour and I was shanghaied (well not really) but I signed aboard the "Monte Cristo"… and so began an interesting year of my life. For some time we moored in Vancouver at the Bayshore hotel and operated as a charter vessel. We took people sailing and often for dinner cruises out beyond the Lions Gate bridge. There were two small cannons on the foredeck that we often fired when we went under the bridge. I got to load them with gunpowder and wads of newspaper and when fired they were very loud and echoed along the bridge. We also went to other places and gave tours of Monte Cristo when we were moored at any wharf. On July 20th

Figure 34 Ralph Eastland in the high rigging, with Luis Dammert below: Seattle Times

1969 we were moored in Nanaimo Harbour and had a hotel room to watch the Apollo 11 landing on the moon on TV. As crew we were not paid much but for the foc'sle crew of 8 sailing a 100 ft barque was a great adventure.

Capt. Gilchrist had studied up on square-rigged ships periodically, in secret. To the crew he kept up a jolly appearance.

Each morning he would greet the young crew with, "Good morning gentlemen! One day closer to the grave." It wasn't known yet that he had misstated his age to the owners by ten years, when he had said he was only sixty-five. The last time he had sailed under canvas had been forty-one years earlier. It had been an auxiliary schooner, whose engine was used at least as much as her sails. ("Auxiliary" meant that an engine was available for use along with the sails.)

The *Cruise Line*'s senior shareholder, Ron Sr., was kept busy scheduling the ship's visits. He had little time to try to replace the old skipper. "Captain Tom'll work into it," was Ron's standard response to questions from the other financial shareholders.

Ron's brother, Fred, had been particularly concerned. "Listen Ron. We are barely making costs with all these excursions along the coast. Gilchrist is not a businessman. He spends our money like a – ok, I have to say it – like a drunken sailor!"

Gilchrist's antics were past laughing at. He would spend all evening and as long into the night as he could in the nearest bar in every port. There, he would talk up the female barkeeper, promising her a position on board as ship's cook if she showed up next morning.

At early light, sure enough, the hapless woman would be dropped off by a taxi, her bags in tow, having given her sudden notice to the bar owner the night before.

She would drag her bags from a taxi to the *Monte Cristo* where one of the patient crew would jump down to the dock to explain to her that they already had a cook and the Captain must have been drunk when he offered her the position. If the crew member was Ron Jr. or Jeff, they would dig into their last few coins to give the poor woman taxi fare back to town.

Fred Craig had been a navigator, flying over 30 missions and later retiring as a Wing commander after commanding at Canadian bases. He had wanted to see action in his investment. His brother Ron was reluctant to rock the boat. "He'll work into it…"

Fred kept asking, "How long are you going to sit by and let Gilchrist play with his toy in this little pond? We have to make the *Charter Line* pay its way!"

Ron nodded. "I'm in contact with some very interesting people in the States, Fred. Captain Tom and the crew need to get their sea-legs, first."

Meanwhile, the *Monte Cristo* sailed into ports along BC's coast, on both sides of the Strait of Georgia. Jeff later wrote:

> It seemed to me that shipping out in *Monte Cristo* was a bit like running away and joining the circus, since the ship was moving from marina to marina with artfully generated publicity. It was the only way that Ron Craig could make her pay at that point. In all, *Monte Cristo* was an impressive vessel, and for all her apparent faults and short-comings I confess to being smitten by her. As with any first love, one tends to overlook her manifest defects. I fell into this honey trap.

They made a grand entrance to Victoria in April 1969. The Inner Harbour was a fitting location, with the imposing provincial Legislature building on one side, and the stately Empress Hotel on the other side, and crowds all around greeting the sailing ship of yore.

Here, Ron Sr. had arranged to have a number of finishing touches applied to the *Monte Cristo* by local craftsmen. At the same time, he made full use of her impressive sails on the front porch of the Legislature, looking to bolster his proposal to support the ship's voyage to Expo '70.

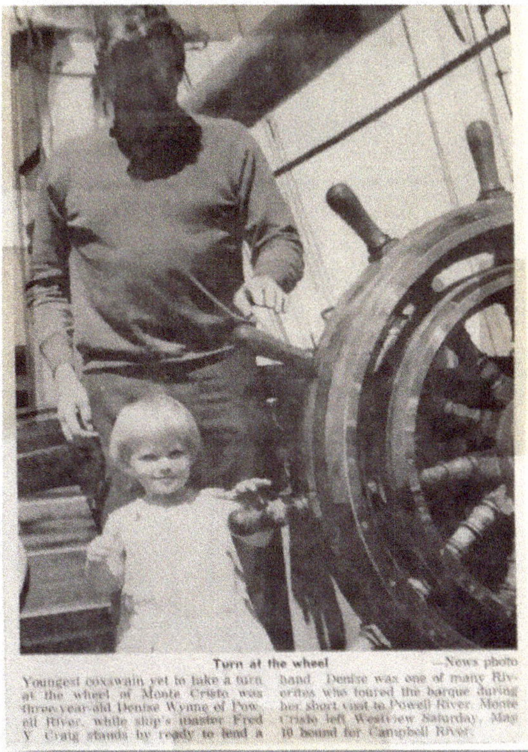

Turn at the wheel —News photo

Youngest coxswain yet to take a turn at the wheel of Monte Cristo was three-year-old Denise Wynne of Powell River, while ship's master Fred V. Craig stands by ready to lend a hand. Denise was one of many Riverites who toured the barque during her short visit to Powell River. Monte Cristo left Westview Saturday, May 10 bound for Campbell River.

Figure 35 Fred Craig and passenger, Powell River

The visit to Powell River in May 1969 brought out crowds who eagerly clambered aboard, for the fee of $2.50 for adults. They would touch the exotic woods, feel the lines and stare all the way up the tall masts.

In August, the *Monte Cristo* was featured at the Nanaimo Bath Tub Race to enthralled crowds. Marine events as far away as Seattle would request the appearance of the *Monte Cristo*.

Having such an impressive ship in the water, however, attracted disputes. If they went to court, the time needed to deal with them, and any losses resulting, kept picking away at the viability of the *Monte Cristo Charter Lines* to make money.

Minor issues with the ship popped up as Gilchrist learned the basic elements of sailing a square-rigger. He became adept at blaming others for his lack of knowledge. During preparations for their first excursion to Seattle, things came to a head on board and between the financial shareholders.

Some of the crew supported Capt. Gilchrist, despite his lack of square-rigger experience and understanding of the special needs of this ship. Most didn't care who was skipper, as long as it was someone in whom they could put their trust. Unwittingly, Jeff Berry became the lightning rod of those who were upset at the disparagement of the skipper, while the rest came to rely on Jeff's practical knowledge of seamanship and navigation.

Stoking the media fires about financial difficulties with the *Monte Cristo Charter Lines*, reporters interrogated crew members when they found them at places they both frequented – at bars. None of the crew knew the details about what the shareholders had been deciding or speaking about in private. That didn't stop them from making up gossip. Even as wild stories

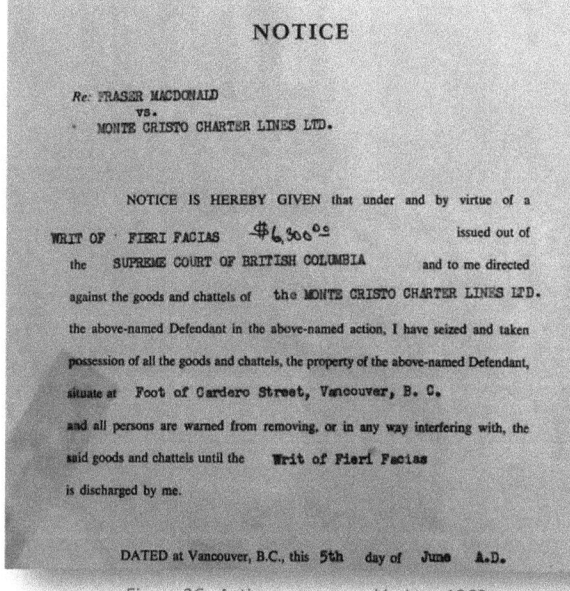

Figure 36 Action commenced in June 1969

were being manufactured about fights in the board room, business plans were being organized by Ron Sr., his brother Fred, and Arnold Brugge. In order to bring the *Monte Cristo's* costs under control they made a decision regarding management. Certain problems would have to be corrected by real marine tradesmen, and Capt. Gilchrist would have to be replaced before long.

At the same time, the vocal minority of the crew who had not wanted change insisted that others were to blame. Gilchrist, who was under pressure by the owners to treat their investment with greater professionalism, had deflected criticism by saying that Jeff Berry had turned the crew against him. The old skipper was finally pushed into a corner. In his mind, he believed he had enough support to get rid of the only person on board who actually knew how to navigate on the ocean and to handle a square-rigger – Jeff.

Figure 37 Monte Cristo Charter Line crest

His opportunity came when Jeff decided to broach the subject of the ship's ballast. He politely asked Capt. Gilchrist, "If I may, sir, can I ask about the stability of the ship? With respect to the ballast…"

Testily, Gilchrist jumped on the point, "There's nothing wrong with her stability and she has been carefully designed to carry exactly this amount of ballast! She sails well and I, personally, checked the ballast. What are you on about?"

An hour later he ordered Jeff to leave the ship. "You, young man, have been causing trouble with my crew and undermining my authority. I will have none of that aboard my ship!"

After a pause, Jeff saluted Capt. Gilchrist, turned and left. He picked up his seabag from below decks and walked away.

A phone call had immediately made this known to Ron Sr. who hurried down to the ship to speak with Jeff in the parking lot.

Making Ready

Ron Sr. was not sure what to say. "Ah, listen Jeff, I'm sorry this had to happen."

" Sir, I was never anything but helpful. Ask the crew. I never once said anything against the Captain. In all my years in the US Navy, one thing you never do is question command."

Ron nodded, "I believe you, Jeff. Let me say this to you in confidence. Captain Tom is on a short leash. It may be that he wants to be rid of anyone of the crew who knows more than he does. As the senior owner, I will tell you that we have not been pleased to have a money-losing operation on our hands. I want you to keep in touch, OK? I may be getting back to you about a job. Where are you going off to now?"

"Thank you, sir. I'll be making my way down to Bremerton, just over the border in Washington. There's a hundred-and-fifty foot steam schooner called the *Explorer* in dry dock. A group of volunteers are working at putting her back together."

Figure 38 *The crew, prior to sailing to the USA, 1969 Mate Ron Jr. is fourth from the right*

Ron Sr. gave Jeff his business card and they shook hands sincerely. "Please stay in touch."

Jeff was called after a short time.

Ron Sr. asked if Jeff was of a mind to return to the *Monte Cristo*.

Jeff told Ron Sr., "Yes, sir. I am still interested. The *Monte Cristo* is my preference. The *Explorer* is going nowhere. Too many pieces lying around and too little cash with which to finish this project. I'm a sailor. Being beached is very frustrating."

Ron Sr. had spoken with Captain Tom and calmed the old man down. There was much work to be done in the background so Ron did not have time right then to play deck politics. It had been agreed that Jeff was to rejoin the crew shortly.

The *Monte Cristo* was set to sail to Bellingham, Washington, and as far into Puget Sound as Olympia. Ron was tapping his connections with the Shriners organization to set up events and publicity all along Puget Sound.

Figure 39 Ballast time

Before sailing into the Sound, however, they first docked at the Lake Union Dry Dock in Washington.

While he had been cooling his heels in Bremerton, Jeff told Ron that he managed to obtain the original invoice from a concrete supplier who had first poured the *Monte Cristo*'s ballast. It turned out that only seven cubic yards had been poured. This equalled fourteen tons, not the twenty-five tons that Brigola and Gilchrist had been telling everybody. The *Monte Cristo* was seriously short regarding stability.

Ron probed Jeff for more information about the ballast and other suggestions to make the ship ready for the high seas.

Jeff could not contain his concern. "My calculations show that the ballast is short by half – at least! When I went down to check the ballast, before he fired me, and I found concrete, I was astonished! For god's sake, you don't pour concrete in place of ballast!"

Ron shook his head blankly. "I'm sorry – I don't understand…"

Breathing deeply to calm down again, "Calculations for ballast are complicated…"

Ron stopped him. "I believe you know what you're talking about, Jeff. Just tell me – why not concrete?"

"The density of concrete is only about 145 pounds per cubic foot. The density of iron, for instance, is over 490 pounds! You can't get anywhere near the amount of concrete into the same space as iron. And now that they've filled the area with concrete, we couldn't fit enough iron shot into her if we wanted to. We could maybe stuff in 15 tons maximum."

Ron had an idea that he should be shocked. But he did not know why. Thinking about it later, he contacted the other owners and convinced them that it was imperative to arrange for a competent facility like Lake Union Dry Dock in Washington state to correct this ballast situation, along with other critical features, before they set out on the open Pacific. The safety of the crew, and any paying passengers, was important!

Thanking Jeff for the technical information, Ron asked Jeff to return to the ship when they docked at Olympia. He was told at that time to keep his head down and stay out of Gilchrist's way until Ron's negotiations and special arrangements could be concluded.

At the busy marine facility north of Seattle, with the *Monte Cristo* out of the water, the crew had a lot time on their hands. Some strutted into town to meet the locals. A few spoke to other mariners in the area to find out more about what might await them on the Pacific.

A neighbour at Lake Union had been Jacques Couseau's ship *Calipso*. Crews visited each other and exchanged stories.

Further upgrades were done here to prepare the ship for a Pacific crossing. More could have been done but money was short.

With the down-time, some crew members had decided to "pay off" – leave the ship.

Figure 40 The Calipso at Lake Union Dry Dock

"...tastic Voyage"

Your ad in the Daily Olympian described exactly that. The sort of thing every man fantasizes about.

The skills and experience I have to offer in a venture such as this span only twenty-three years, vary and may seem not to apply in this case.

I served honorably in the United States Navy as a deck and weapons crew member.

Figure 41 Request to join the crew

Finding more crew members meant that Ron was regularly posting advertisements in the newspapers of cities they were coming to. The replies were sorted, then the better ones were given to the captain for a final judgement.

By September 1969, the *Monte Cristo* was refloated. They set off to a rendezvous in Seattle.

One of the surprises that Ron had been arranging was a face-off between the *Monte Cristo* and the world's largest battleship, the *New Jersey* (BB-62).

It wasn't a fair fight. The *Monte Cristo* got off the only shots.

This was just before the battleship's third decommissioning, so her mighty guns were silenced. Ron had set up the display so that media would capture the *Monte Cristo*'s two little deck cannons going pop-pop (with blanks) in the shadow of the *New Jersey*. It did feature prominently in the news media.

Figure 42 Captured by the New Jersey

Ron and the crew were then invited on board the *New Jersey*.

Ralph Eastland remembered this time:

> Monte Cristo always attracted lots of attention wherever we went. In July we stopped at Oak Bay [Victoria] for some time and then headed south into Puget Sound. The American rules for charter vessels prevented us from chartering but we could offer tours of the boat so we visited several ports on our way to Seattle for a refit. The crew worked on replacing worn parts of the rigging while moored in Seattle, but we also went sailing in Puget Sound. One day a battleship, "USS *New Jersey*" was passing Seattle returning from Vietnam to Tacoma to be decommissioned so we sailed out to have a look. She was 900 ft in length and as we sailed by her we fired our two cannons. Of course our firing was really a salute... I remember standing in front of one of the 16 inch guns and marvelling at the motto "Firepower for Freedom" that was painted on the housing. One of the crew told me that our cannons were the only time that they had been fired upon since they left for Vietnam. When they were there the boat sat offshore and fired at targets 20 miles inland.

Figure 43 *Captain Peniston and Ron C. Craig*

Taking advantage of the great publicty, Ron arranged for his ship to dock in Seattle. The owners wanted to test the market for corporate charters. It did not prove as lucrative as expected.

One of the crew, Bill Mitchell, remembers Seattle:

> We spent much of the summer docked in Seattle in front of Ye Olde Curiosity Shoppe. None of the crew was paid (at least not as far as I knew) and we covered our costs by giving guided tours of *Monte Cristo* and taking groups out for a sail in the harbour. Usually we would bring in enough to buy our food for the day, I only have vague memories about who acted as cook, and some days we ate better than others. I also remember walking around Seattle in bare feet to toughen the soles of my feet for climbing the rigging. This was a time when the Vietnam War was in full swing and one day a bus driver asked me if I was trying to get flat feet to get out of the draft, to which I answered 'No, I'm Canadian', possibly followed by a longer explanation.

The sojourn in Seattle was also memorable to Ralph Eastland:

> We were tied up close to downtown Seattle for most of the time that we were there. Of course there was work to be done but we had lots of free time in port. The bottom maintenance and heavier work was to be done at a shipyard, so we went up the channel and through the locks to Lake Union where *Monte Cristo* was hauled out of the water and those things were taken care of while the crew worked on our own projects including replacing much of the running rigging... Work done and relaunched, we proceeded further inland to Lake Washington to watch the unlimited hydroplane races.
>
> *Monte Cristo* was tied to a string of boomsticks that surrounded the racecourse so we had better seats than the helicopter since we were closer to the action. The crew climbed into the rigging to watch from higher up than the deck. Those hydroplanes skipped sideways across the water so much as they raced around the course they came close to hitting us. *Miss Budweiser* was the

winner.

We also got to drive to Tacoma for the drag boat races. A boat named *Miss British Columbia* was the fastest, covering the quarter mile racecourse in 8 seconds. In 1969 she was the world record holder at 192 miles/hr. She burned some kind of fuel made

Figure 44 *Crew Aloft*

from nitro glycerine and the owner said the engine would explode if he didn't stop after ten seconds. Don't know if that was true but it was something to watch! *Monte Cristo* could do 12 knots sailing under perfect conditions.

Other activities like sailing small boats and seeing the sights also kept us entertained in the Seattle area. Roger and I rented a sailing dingy in Lake Union and were almost hit by a seaplane that landed a short distance away. We left Seattle to head south for San Francisco at the end of summer which proved to be a dangerous and exciting decision.

A nagging thing hadn't been formally stated by the crew on board: a few of the sailors were not paid as seamen but were, themselves, paying for the privilege of sailing on the *Monte Cristo*. The owners had sold berths to part of the crew and paid the others as regular seamen. Even though this had not been openly discussed while in Puget Sound, it created an undercurrent of muttered discontent that kept the crew from being a coordinated team.

The lack of effective training in their complicated tasks had driven another wedge between some crew members. This situation would fester as they sailed through, then out of Puget Sound, until it came to a head in January of next year.

Figure 45   Seattle Times July 1969

Are We Ready?

Ron had spoken more than once with Jeff prior to the ship's leaving the southern part of Puget Sound, at Olympia, Washington. He needed honest answers about his ship.

"I'm arranging for a staff photographer from National Geographic to be on board from Seattle to San Francisco. He is going to be taking pictures all the way and I need to know if the ship is up to the coastal seas, Jeff. I don't want the wrong kind of pictures to be taken. What needs working on before we go through the Strait of Juan de Fuca?"

Jeff always went right to the point. It was a disconcerting trait to those who preferred small talk. "Thank you for asking, sir. The *Monte Cristo* has a number of serious flaws. The auxiliary does no more than paddle the water under the stern – nowhere near enough power. The rudder was not sized to affect her helm as it needs to."

Ron started taking notes but his pen slowed down and stopped with the number of points that Jeff brought up.

"She has few mechanical systems. No refrigeration, no generator, no efficient bilge pumping system, no small boats and no authorized safety gear. There is, on a positive note, a crystal-controlled double-band transceiver with a 200-mile range, at night. Workable, under good conditions."

Jeff went on. "And then there's the bigger issue of the masts' locations. Little can be done at this time to correct that, short of a major rebuild. It looks like Alex didn't base his calculations on the waterline, as an experienced marine architect does. Where they placed the masts causes mainmast yards to foul against the foremast lines. That will require special training of the crew to avoid problems on the open sea. Aloft, there are some really horrid foul leads in the rigging. Nothing's been tarred, so the material will weather too quickly. Manila lanyards secure the standing rigging…"

He looked up at Ron to see a confused expression.

Jeff explained, "Standing rigging secures the masts in their proper alignment against the forces of the wind. Manila stretches when wet, then breaks. Not a good choice for lanyards that are intended to maintain stability between the masts. And, my god! – crew training! First of all, six seamen is the minimum you need for a few hours on English Bay. To sail the Pacific you need to double that – for the two watches. And while this crew is eager to learn, you don't take a complex vessel like a square-rigger onto the Pacific without detailed and repeated training in all the important tasks they have to be able to execute immediately on command. Remember what happened that first time we set out for Nanaimo?"

Ron was getting concerned. "But we just spent thousands of dollars on the ballast and rudder and other things you said she needed!"

Jeff nodded. "We will have to do what can be done while we sail down the coast."

On the way north through Puget Sound, yet one of the issues in the ship showed itself. They had to breast the Sound's formidable tidal currents, particularly past the Tacoma Narrows, which actually swept them backwards. The *Monte Cristo* could not carry on until after the tide ebbed. Jeff later wrote,

> I think the ancient Buda diesel originally produced about seventy-five horsepower. However, from the anemic way it ran, I was sure that half of those horses had died long before. In still water it would push the *Monte Cristo* slightly faster than four knots. The tidal current in the Narrows often raced at *six* knots when it ebbed.

Ron departed with his notes and much to do. His son, Ron Jr. was no longer aboard. It would be up to Jeff Berry to communicate with Ron. Captain Tom couldn't be trusted to give a straight answer.

Are We Ready?

Ron was working very hard to make the *Monte Cristo Cruise Line* pay its way. He was constantly promoting the ship as a unique weekend getaway for businesses. Several interesting projects were also in the works. Publicity was ever Ron's forte.

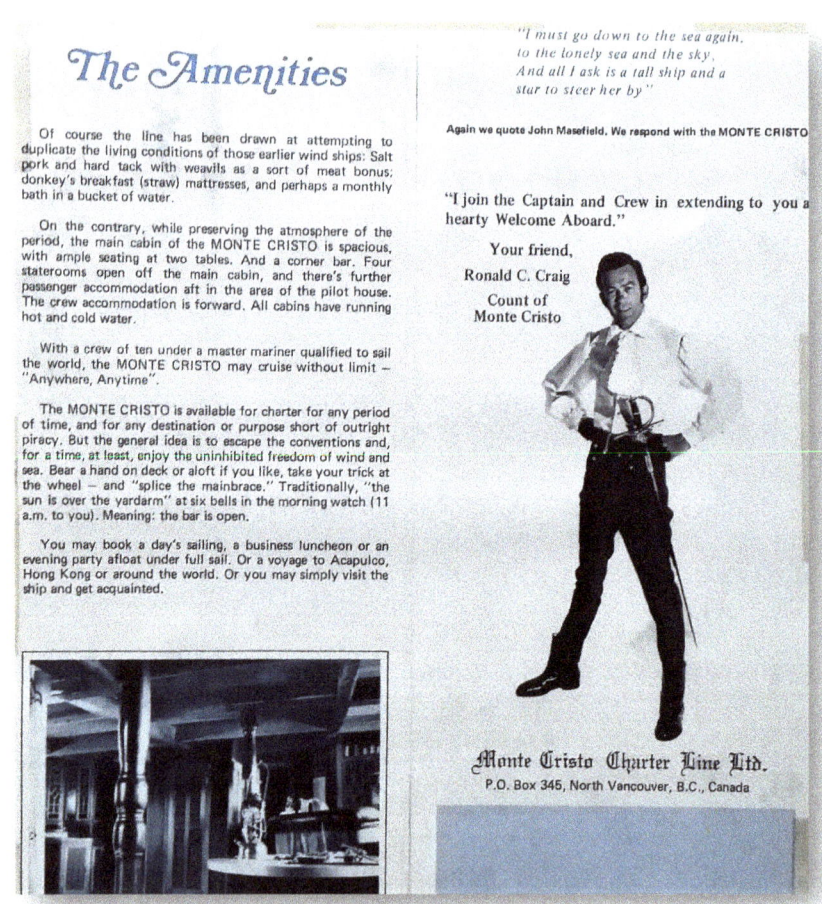

Figure 46 Promotion brochure

Sailing through the Strait of Juan de Fuca, heading for the Pacific and down the coast to San Francisco, they were delayed.

The weather was calm. So calm, in fact, that Gilchrist gave up on canvas and ordered the auxiliary "lit" (turned on).

Are We Ready?

The lack of wind was combined with an untrained crew, plus turbulent currents in the strait, all of which caught the *Monte Cristo* with her skirt down. The bow and stern alternately dipped into the swells with such force that water smashed into the engine's exhaust pipe, flooding it with cold salt water. The old diesel chugged bravely then coughed to a full stop.

The jibs and spanker sails were unfurled, prayers were uttered in suitably salty tones, and the ship was coaxed over to the American side of the strait toward Neah Bay. Putting pride aside, a tow into the harbour was requested. A Coast Guard boat hauled the ship to dock, where the diesel was repaired.

Ralph Eastland recalled that incident:

> On my birthday we were crossing Juan De Fuca Strait and had an engine problem. That was when I learned that I was not prone to seasickness. I spent several hours head down in the diesel fumes trying to repair the engine while we drifted in the fog only to eventually be towed into Port Townsend for repairs.

The Captain's and crew's inexperience had nearly caused the *Monte Cristo*, once again, to have an inauspicious meeting with Davey Jones. Conversing earnestly in his cabin with a bottle of whiskey, Captain Tom convinced himself that, once the engine was repaired, the sails should stay furled on the way down to San Francisco. And so it happened.

Ron Craig was not at all pleased with the added cost of diesel fuel. He had promised the other shareholders that wind was free and costs would be minimal.

Like a Hobby-Horse

The run down the Pacific coast to San Francisco was pleasant enough. Finally past the waters of Juan de Fuca, on turning south at Cape Flattery the charts showed a prohibited area to avoid, along with a number of other navigational complications. This forced Gilchrist to ask for assistance from Jeff. With his navigational experience in the US Navy, Jeff was easily able to chart a course that would take them south of Oregon.

On the second day, Jeff was in the rigging with one of the non-farmer crew members known as *Lucky*. Looking at the poorly furled sails and flapping canvas, Jeff shook his head in the manner of Captain Cook.

"This is not going to last."

Lucky had been hanging tightly onto two ratlines and was, nevertheless, being swung roughly in grand arcs with each long swell. He replied with a distracted, "What?"

"The canvas; the rigging; the hardware... It is all too

Figure 47 Motoring, with canvas flapping

loose. With every sway, the canvas and the lines wear away. And the hardware is pulled…" Jeff suddenly stopped, staring up at the royals, then down to the deck.

Lucky let out another, "What?"

Jeff thought briefly, then, "I see. Now I know why this ship is so hard to work."

With an arm secured to a stay, he explained to Lucky, "The *Monte Cristo* hobby-horses more than any ship I've been on. I thought it was merely a function of the square sails, but that's only part of it."

A heavier swell rose and sent them sharply aft then flung them forward.

"There! You see how much she pitches?"

"AHH!" Lucky lost his firm grip as one of the ratlines was looser than the others. Regaining his hold, the young sailor moved in closer to Jeff for greater stability. He tempted fate by looking down from their precarious height. "Pitches. Yes. A lot."

Nodding, Jeff assumed the professorial tone that the Saskatchewan farmers on the crew perceived as being aloof. "There is too much canvas and the *Monte Cristo* does not need royals, and perhaps not even t'gallants. It has to do with her waterline, the shape of the keel and the vessel's sail area."

Lucky rolled his eyes as Jeff indicated upward then down. But, other than holding on tightly, he had nothing better to do than to listen.

Jeff continued, "A square-rig design gives a vessel the largest possible sail area per mast. The press of sail on the foremast pushes the bow down. Combined with the unusual rounded keel shape that Brigola chose – there is far less run than there should be."

Lucky started to get interested. "What do you mean by run?"

Like a Hobby-Horse

"That is the length of the keel at the point of maximum beam. If the keel was straight, not bowed, it would better support the hull uniformly along the waterline. What we have is, in effect, the stability of a football bobbing on water rather than a yard-stick floating on it. And with the taller masts, the effect of every swell is to swing the high point of the masts across a much longer arc."

Having worked in a factory, Lucky had a good practical understanding of mechanical principles. He nodded, "So when we're up on the royal yard, we swing over twenty feet with each swell… that's why!"

"Right. Lots of fun in a drizzle, too. Now, add to that effect the lack of buoyancy of the cutwater…"

"The bow?"

"Yes. The shape of the bow was chosen – again, I don't know why Brigola would have done this, except that it *looked* nice – the bow slices into the waves, then is pushed down by the press of sail. The excessive overhang – yet another lovely cosmetic addition – slaps into the water and forces the bow back up quickly. A similar effect occurs at the stern with another cosmetic addition of fancy skirts that, I suppose, were added to visually balance the extended bow."

Engaged in the discussion, Lucky added, "So that's why she doesn't, ah, hobby-horse so much with sails furled and we motor along!"

"Right. And that may be why the captain instinctively is keeping the sails furled as we sail down-coast. Furled as much as the crew is able."

Lucky caught on to what Jeff was saying earlier. "You mean that with the canvas not being tightly furled, we're both hobby-horsing more than we should when we motor, and the material is being worn faster."

"Correct."

Nodding in agreement. "Well, we could just say that only the dandies can work the sails above the main yard."

Jeff looked sternly at Lucky. "That is not a term I want to hear any more. Everybody on board is a seaman. We all pull our own weight. If some have chosen to pay for the privilege of sailing under canvas, it does not diminish their contribution on the high seas. We cannot have that kind of division among the crew."

Head down, "Sorry. You're right, I suppose. Jeez, you sound like a skipper."

Hobby-horsing, the *Monte Cristo* carried on through light swells and occasional showers all the way to San Francisco.

As will happen in a group under some stress, two main cliques formed below deck. There were those who now proudly called themselves seamen, having made it all the way from the Prairies, to Burrard Inlet, into Puget Sound, then out into the actual Pacific Ocean – well, the northwest coast, anyway. They had signed on as crew for a very meagre salary. It was the experience that counted!

In addition to the farmers and Lucky, there were four crew members still on board who had been convinced by Ron Craig to pay their way on this adventure. These crew members took part in all the duties aloft but, having paid for a bunk, they felt they deserved a few concessions below deck. The two cliques were careful not to get into outright fights, most of the time. Nevertheless, the tension between them made for a less than optimal situation when Captain Tom piped out an order to "hoist the royals". Scampering around lines that were cold and slippery, at heights that were dizzying, put folks on edge. Only the bravest would climb high, Jeff Berry among them, to unfurl sails at a time when it was much wiser to just motor along.

Jeff had been relied on more often to help Gilchrist steer a course away from the jagged parts of the coast. It was a balancing act of staying within sight but not too close to rocks. The occasional fog complicated things.

Everybody was anxious to get to the safety of San Francisco harbour. Captain Gilchrist had been stretched beyond his capabilities and snapped at anyone in his way. He badly needed to see the bottom of a fresh whiskey bottle.

On shore, Ron Craig had been fighting through the heavier storms raised by his fellow owners, including his brother, Fred.

Ron was promising a bountiful take in the land of rich corporations. He deflected calls to turn the *Monte Cristo* around and sell her off. His goal, instead, was San Francisco's famous Pier 39. At Fisherman's Wharf, he promised, the public would flock aboard.

Figure 48 Approaching San Francisco

San Francisco

Passing Mendocino in October, 1969, tension among the crew had been rising and they had been getting tired of the late fall's chilly weather.

One thing was now on their mind. The word spread that, sailing hard, they would be able to make San Francisco next day.

However, Captain Tom ordered Jeff to plot a course into Mendocino. He wanted to take on a few supplies, give the crew a breather, and clean the ship before showing up in the big city. Also, and perhaps more critically, he needed the services of a bar.

Jeff had to politely explain that there were no facilities for the *Monte Cristo* at Mendocino. They would not be able to dock there.

Captain Tom swore at Jeff, "What do you mean we can't dock there? Damn you, you just want the crew to get mad at me, don't you?"

He stomped off to his cabin to find the last of his supply of whiskey.

Shaking his head at the old captain, Jeff stayed at the plotting table and was at hand when Ron Craig called via the wireless.

"Shall I fetch Captain Gilchrist for you?"

"No. No need. You know what we spoke about earlier. I'm in San Francisco now. Arranging for you to tie up at Pier 39. On my own, here. My contacts have all decided to follow the sun down to Palm Springs. Have to work things out. Don't worry…" He left instructions to be passed to Captain Gilchrist.

"See you there tomorrow."

Next day, the *Monte Cristo* was sailing in clearer weather along the Bonita Channel, heading southeast for the entrance to San Francisco Bay.

Jeff strongly advised against using the narrow channel. The standard approach was to sail around the shallow Fourfathom Bank when approaching from the north, then join the main shipping lane from the southwest.

Captain Tom was insistent. "No! We are taking the direct route! I'm damned if I'm going under the Golden Gate Bridge in the evening! Nobody will see us."

Indeed, Ron Craig asked Jeff to leave a message for Captain Tom to say that reporters and their photographers had been alerted to be ready for the *Monte Cristo* as she sailed, with canvas unfurled, under the orange bridge. No amount of polite explanation to either Ron or Captain Tom could convince them of the dangers the ship faced on that shallower route. Publicity was very important!

As it happened, few photographers were in a position to capture the *Monte Cristo* sailing under the Golden Gate Bridge.

It was raining as they passed into the Bay, going by little Alcatraz Island. Having been closed down a few years previously, the former penitentiary island looked cold, forlorn and rusting away, sitting solitary inside the Bay's entrance.

> Up in the luffing main royal sail, the visage of Captain Cook might have been seen smiling. The *Monte Cristo* was to have an adventure in those waters shortly.

They made as grand an entrance into the harbour as they could. Ron Craig was on Pier 39 with a small welcoming party of media as the sailing ship made her tentative approach under power and with only two jibs and the spanker unfurled.

Seasoned sailors saw what the general public did not – this ship's crew did not know how to furl sails, nor when to do it. And, on closer examination some wondered aloud at the "Irish pennants" in the rigging (loose flapping ends of lines).

Ever the one for promotion, Ron dressed as his version of a pirate captain, calling himself the *Count of Monte Cristo*. The public was drawn by his showmanship and the ship's impressive masts so that respectable numbers of the public paid to visit the ship over the following days.

San Francisco had a long history of sailing. The square-rigger did draw old salts to her at Pier 39.

"Jesus! Will you look at that, Charlie! I was on one of these ships before you were born!"

Figure 49 Ron Sr. as Captain Cook

His friend replied, "Right. That would explain those face wrinkles of yours that look treacherous enough to fall into!"

Another sailing vessel was docked nearby. It was the *Balclutha*, under the command of a legend in the sailing fraternity, Captain Ip Riis.

While Captain Tom took the first opportunity to scurry off to find the nearest sailor's bar, Jeff walked over to the *Balclutha*. Talking with the seasoned captain, Jeff then asked permission to climb up into the rigging where he took copious notes.

Next day, Jeff told Ron Craig about Captain Riis. They both went back to the *Balclutha* to speak with him.

Jeff wrote about that time:

San Francisco

Capt. Ip Riis, then master of *Balclutha*, was most helpful. A Dane, he had sailed in several of the Grain Race ships from Australia to Europe before and immediately after World War II. Captain Riis boarded *Monte Cristo* and showed us how to put a harbour furl on our ill-fitting sails. He confirmed to the owner that the ship was severely under ballasted, and that Gilchrist was not completely candid in his qualifications.

When they had hired him, Ron Craig had taken Tom Gilchrist at his word. Capt. Riis was compelled to give a less than complementary story, as remembered by Jeff:

> The most interesting thing Riis told Craig was that, when he and Gilchrist had been in their cups in the wee hours that morning, Captain Gilchrist had admitted he was actually born in 1894, not 1904. Some place along the line he had managed to lose a decade when his last license had been issued. Our captain was actually seventy-five years old! The chronology of

Figure 50 San Francisco – sails are finally ship-shape

San Francisco

some of his sea stories all fell into place then.

More publicity for the Monte Cristo was arranged for the next day when Ron ordered Gilchrist to take the ship out for three short sails on the Bay. It had been then that an angry Ron Craig saw the old captain nursing a whiskey bottle on deck. Gilchrist made a half-hearted attempt to hide it from the media people near him.

Seeing a quick slurp of whiskey, Ron grabbed his arm and whispered roughly, "Are you out of your mind! What do you think you're doing with that bottle?"

Gilchrist was defensive. "Ah, come now, Mr. Craig. Every sailor takes a drink." He then made the mistake of adding, "And we've closed more than one bar, you and I."

"Not in sight of the press and Fisherman's Wharf, we haven't! When the *Monte Cristo* is underway you will be sober!"

Gilchrist replied contritely, "Yes sir. Absolutely right. I should know better than to put the ship in jeopardy. I promise you that I shall be on my best behaviour in San Francisco."

The next night Gilchrist found different sailor's bar. Before the place closed for the night he had hired yet another cook.

That morning, it was Ron Craig who had to tell the unfortunate woman that the captain had made a mistake. That was one cook too many.

On sending the unfortunate woman on her way, Ron turned and yelled down below for Gilchrist to be wakened. He was fired on the spot.

Jeff sadly recalled that event:

> The Scot disappeared into his cabin and soon we heard the taps of his portable typewriter in action as he banged out scathing letters to other stockholders of the *Monte Cristo Company*, complaining of his mistreatment. Worse came. Captain Gilchrist

decided I had engineered his fall. This was absolutely false. He had done it all without any help or push from anyone else. I had merely observed this Shakespearean tragedy evolve episode by episode. I had never ratted on him or betrayed him in any way. I was not even the mate on the ship and never challenged Gilchrist for his job for the simple reason that I didn't want his responsibility so soon. To be sure, I wanted to be a sailing ship master some day, but not necessarily the *Monte Cristo* and not then. I knew that I was unqualified to command at that stage in my career. I still regret that Capt. Thomas Gilchrist blamed me for his removal. I tried to talk to him about it, but he wouldn't listen to me. After all these years, I can only conclude what I thought on the day this happened: that a good man had been laid low by the passage of years. He was angry that his body no longer reacted the way he wanted it to. He therefore took a dog in the manger attitude and did his damnedest to make certain that he was the one oracle of wisdom on matters nautical for *Monte Cristo*. As long as he was visiting small fishing ports on Vancouver Island, or in Puget Sound, he got away with it. However, in San Francisco, there was a reservoir of sailing knowledge. Instead of embracing this opportunity to bone up on sailing technique, he tried to brazen out his shortcomings. In all, it was a sorry business. He should have known when to quit gracefully. I resolved that when my time came, as it does to us all, I would try to make an elegant exit.

The next morning, I awoke to find that the mate and half the Canadian crew had left; on their own or urged by Gilchrist, I don't know. The four remaining hands started calling me Skipper, a title I didn't seek, but short of quitting myself, I could not duck.

I spoke to Ron Craig, who asked me to take command until he could find someone with proper sail endorsement papers. This would be required if we were ever to take passengers for hire... We could only have parties alongside and free cruises in American waters, in any case, because of Jones Act restrictions. I agreed to stay long enough for him to find that right person.

I was twenty-seven years old, suddenly master under God of a 3-masted barque, with a wonky engine, many faults, unseasoned crewmembers and an owner who wanted her to make him some money.

On the main royal yard Captain Cook nodded and mouthed, "Finally."

Ron Craig was left with less than half a crew and an untested skipper. He went quietly back to speak with Captain Riis. Directed to the same seaman's bar where they had met previously, Ron found Riis sitting with another captain.

Coming up to the table, Riis smiled and introduced Ron to his companion.

"James, this is the fellow who owns that lovely barque. Ron Craig. James is the skipper of, shall I say, a venerable sloop docked on the west side Fisherman's Wharf."

Ron detected a quick grin at the word "lovely".

"My pleasure, James." They shook hands. "Captain Riis may be too kind in calling the *Monte Cristo* lovely." Ron wasn't sure how to take the banter.

James was polite but Captain Riis was a forthright man. "My apologies, Ron. I will admit that the lines of the *Monte Cristo* were somewhat perplexing to us when we first saw the ship. Your new skipper, Jeff Berry, explained to me the peculiarities in her construction. You have an excellent man, there. I predict he will do as good a job as anyone can."

Ron had wondered how he was going to ease into the fact that Tom Gilchrist had been fired but it seemed that the dockside chatter travelled faster than a speedboat.

"So you've heard already?"

They both nodded.

"And you know that I will need a skipper with qualifications."

Riis wasted no time in telling Ron what needed saying. "Listen. Your ship needs serious repairs before you attempt setting out past the harbour. Jeff has all my recommendations. What can be done here, what *must* be done, is to make the ship safe. There are design details that Jeff can make accommodations for, and the second main need she has will be addressed by training. Your crew is in dire need of training. The farmers may be willing but they are just not up to it."

Ron nodded. "Yes, well, about that – the farmers and the first mate have left."

"Good," Riis emphasized with a hard slap of the table. "Now, Ron, you and Jeff must select from the real seamen to be found here and from down the coast to San Diego."

James added, with Riis agreeing to help, "I will put the word out. The *Monte Cristo* needs sailors."

San Francisco

Figure 51 Monte Cristo, port side

San Francisco

Let's Invade Alcatraz

Figure 52 from Alcatraz! Alcatraz! by Adam Fortunate Eagle

A few blocks away from Fisherman's Wharf and the interested crowd around the *Monte Cristo*, a set of events had been happening that would soon merge with the ship on Pier 39.

Some days before, the San Francisco Indian Center had burned down. It had been the focal point for a wide grouping of young people who had come to San Francisco from Indian tribes from across the country, even Alaska. Under the Council's elected Chairman, Adam Fortunate Eagle, and after much deliberation, it was decided that the group should make a bold statement about the deplorable conditions they had all experienced in their respective homelands. Rather than strike out in unfocused anger, Adam had channeled their energies toward an action that was calculated to wake up their oppressors. They would make a peaceful invasion of Alcatraz.

The penitentiary island had been closed for several years. A caretaker was generally the only occupant. As barren as the Rock was, it represented the lands callously taken away from its first inhabitants. Once the island's utility had ended, it was left to rot.

A well-thought out proclamation was developed under the signature, *Indians of All Tribes*. The day for invasion was set for November 9th. Supplies were purchased and five boats were rented to take the party across the bay to Alcatraz. Media had been briefed, though sworn to secrecy until the event was to occur.

In the words of Adam Fortunate Eagle, in his book *Alcatraz! Alcatraz!*, that morning was beautiful and calm:

> Feeling optimistic, we were soon on the Nimitz Freeway heading for Fisherman's Wharf and Pier 39 in San Francisco. I began thinking that we were doing a pretty strange thing. 20th-century urban Indians who had gathered in tribal councils, student organizations, and clubs, were now gathering with concerned individuals from all over the Bay Area to launch an attack on a bastion of the United States Government. Instead of riding horses and carrying bows, arrows, and rifles, we were riding in Fords, Chevys, and Plymouths and carrying only our proclamation and determination to change the federal policy oppressing our people.

> We paid our 50 cents to cross the Bay Bridge and even got a friendly wave from the toll collector as we continued on our way, taking in the beauty of the scene. Ahead on our right lay Treasure Island, and we could see the Golden Gate further across the bay on the western horizon. South of the bridge lay the sprawl of the city of San Francisco, and to the north rose the purplish hills of Mann County, with Angel Island snuggled up to its shore. Amidst all this natural and man-made beauty sat the forlorn and neglected little island of Alcatraz—our destination.

The closer Adam and his family drove to Pier 39, the greater their tension rose:

> We were nearing Fisherman's Wharf; smells of the delicious seafood for which the wharf is famous filled the air. As we pulled up to the dock we could see several Indians and a couple of television crews milling around. We were greeted by shouts. "Where the hell are the boats?" The first sign of trouble.
>
> As calmly as possible I replied, "They are supposed to be over by the Harbor Tours dock. There should be about five of them."
>
> "Nope. There ain't a damn thing there next to the wharf except the Harbor Tours boat. The bastards must've chickened out!" They sure had. Everyone was worried and angry.
>
> Another worried voice exclaimed, "Jesus Christ! We've got to find ourselves a boat or we're in big trouble with the press—those guys will tear us up!"
>
> I hurriedly parked the car and ran over to the growing group of Indian students. I asked them to keep everyone occupied by stalling for time any way they could while we went looking for another boat. Richard Oakes asked if they could read the Proclamation; it would take a bit of time and he felt the need for more participation by the students from San Francisco State. I handed him a copy.
>
> He and his group set out for the end of the pier, the other

Let's Invade Alcatraz

Indians and the television crews following. The students settled down in a clearing of benches and planters with Alcatraz Island as a hazy backdrop—a perfect setting for an outdoor press conference. With that diversion begun, we directed our attention to finding a boat.

Desperate for a boat, Adam looked up and down Pier 39. Perhaps the visage of Captain Cook shimmering on a royal yard caught Adam's eye.

> As I stood on the wharf I watched a beautiful three-masted barque that looked like it had come right out of the pages of maritime history. It was named the *Monte Cristo*. I watched the crew members go about their tasks under the observant eye of a handsome man with an air of authority. He had to be either the captain or the owner. From a distance, his tight pants, ruffled shirt, and long hair made him look like Errol Flynn in an adventure movie. I later learned that his name was Ronald Craig and he was the owner of the beautiful vessel.
>
> Still wearing my full tribal dress, I began to approach him. He called over to me, "Hey, I'm curious. What's going on over there with all those Indians?" I didn't hesitate for a minute, because I realized he could be our solution.

Adam introduced himself to Ron Craig. Politely, he asked if it was possible that the *Monte Cristo* could be rented for an excursion on San Francisco Bay. Ron's ears perked up right away.

> He stood deliberating this request. He looked at the whole scene: a growing crowd of Indian men, women and children, all wearing different tribal outfits; the news media with their paraphernalia; and curious bystanders and tourists who waited out of anticipation for something to happen. He looked at his ship, then looked again at the Indians. I held my breath. Finally he spoke.
>
> "I'll do it on the condition that we get permission from the Coast

> Guard to put out to sea and that we take no more than 50 people aboard. The boat rides deep in the water because of the keel, so I can't land on the Alcatraz dock. We'll just circle the island a couple of times, if that's all right with you. Just a sort of sight-seeing tour to get your message across, okay?"
>
> Was it okay? Man alive! At this point I was ready to accept a kayak and he wanted to know if his offer was okay!

Ron called Jeff over to explain what he needed from the Coast Guard. As Jeff was ex-Navy and an American, he would know what to say.

A call was made via the wireless and Jeff returned quickly to Ron.

"I asked whether we would be permitted to carry a large group of passengers for a brief excursion."

"Did you say they were Indians?"

"No sir. They are simply passengers, like any other."

Ron searched for a smile but Jeff was fully serious.

"We have been given permission to do that, providing there are no more than fifty non-paying passengers and it does not last more than the day."

> (Adam) ran back to the wharf to share the good news. Worried looks quickly turned into big smiles as word spread among the Indians and here and there a whoop of joy went up from the crowd.
>
> In a rush, we all converged on the *Monte Cristo*. In no time her decks were awash with Indians, reporters, photographers, and even some of the curious bystanders who came along for whatever adventure lay ahead. But we quickly realized that we had far more than 50 people. Captain Craig approached me shaking his head.

"We can't shove off with this many people aboard," he warned, "the Coast Guard will never let us cast off at this rate."

A number of disappointed people were told they needed to leave until Jeff's head-count had approximately fifty passengers on board.

Sailing out to Alcatraz, Adam remembered thinking:

> What a strange turnabout of history. Here were nearly 50 Indians on an old sailing vessel, heading out to seek a new way of life for their people. I thought of the Mayflower and its crew of Pilgrims who had landed on our shores 350 years earlier. The history books say they were seeking new freedom for themselves and their children, freedom denied them in their homeland.

And so it happened that the *Monte Cristo* took the fifty people out for a free cruise to Alcatraz island. They circled the rocky place twice. Adam Fortunate Eagle and his people stared longingly over the 100 yards of choppy waters to the rocky shore. Finally, one brave could not contain himself any longer. He tore off everything but his pants and jumped overboard.

When he saw the man leap, Ron Craig yelled out, "NO!"

One of the passengers, an Eskimo, shook his head. "Not good."

Jeff was nearby and saw what had concerned the expert in ocean waters. The current around Alcatraz was strengthening. It would tend to pull the swimmer *away* from the island.

Yelling out a stern order, Jeff headed for the crowd, "No more! It's too dangerous!" He had to stop others from jumping.

Ron yelled at Adam, "You can't do this! We're flying the Canadian flag! They'll say we are invading American territory!"

Despite attempts to stop them, three more people jumped overboard and started swimming for all they were worth. Jeff ordered the engine stopped but they could not risk approaching any closer to the rocky shore.

Let's Invade Alcatraz

To everyone's great relief, all four "invaders" managed to fight their way through the cold waves and onto the rocks. They gathered strength and stood up to wave to the ship and nearby media boats. The invasion of Alcatraz was underway.

Another small boatload with ten people then slipped in to the island's dock. The invasion force started with fourteen. It was later to be increased. The government blustered and threatened and took measures against the group for another year-and-a-half before

The Indians came twice by sea; the first time they rode the barque Monte Cristo

Figure 53   from article by Tim Findley, San Francisco Examiner

Alcatraz once more came under the control of the United States of America. Jeff clearly remembered the event:

> It was one hellva baptism of command. That morning, Craig and I spied some American Indians in full buckskin and feathered regalia walking along Fishermen's Wharf. They boarded *Monte Cristo* and asked Craig if they could charter her for a cruise. Ron

explained that we couldn't charter in American waters. Too bad, they replied. We only want to circle Alcatraz Island, shake our fists at the prison and denounce the American Government for keeping The Rock, when they should rightfully give it back to us Native Americans.

Ron had wanted publicity and he received it in spades. Newspaper reporters along with radio and television crews had all been primed

Figure 54 Media coverage - San Francisco Examiner

for the invasion. The media had a field day.

Motoring back to Pier 39, the *Monte Cristo* was accompanied by an upset Coast Guard ship.

As soon as they tied up, Federal Agents boarded and demanded that the skipper and owner explain themselves.

With the passengers still walking off the ship, a red-faced agent fairly spit his questions at Ron Craig and Jeff Berry, "You! You two in charge?" Both nodded. "I want to know *right now*, what deal you made with these Indians?"

Ron responded as calmly as he could, "Nothing. We made no deal. Not a penny changed hands. They merely wanted to cruise, for free, around Alcatraz."

At that the agent turned to accost one of the departing passengers, "You! How much did you pay for this trip?"

Shaking his head suspiciously at the Agent, "Didn't pay anything."

That served to rile the agent more. "You're lying! Tell me how much you was charged!"

The passenger shook his head and turned away.

The agent could barely contain himself. He spun around to yell something more at Ron but the vision of an angelic Errol Flynn-like sea captain standing calmly before him was disconcerting to the agent. He took a few heavy breaths. "So you didn't know what these Indians was doing?"

Ron had his friendly cherub face on. "No sir. We've been in front of Fisherman's Wharf for a couple days to get publicity for our grand sailing ship. The only way we can feed the crew is to have people pay to come on board, while moored, to tour

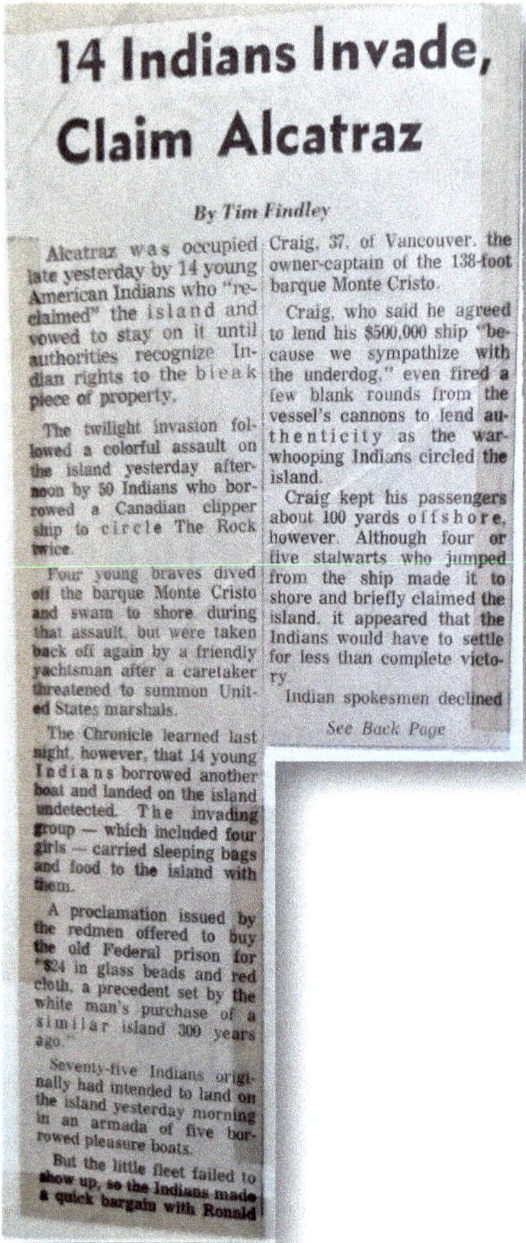

14 Indians Invade, Claim Alcatraz

By Tim Findley

Alcatraz was occupied late yesterday by 14 young American Indians who "reclaimed" the island and vowed to stay on it until authorities recognize Indian rights to the bleak piece of property.

The twilight invasion followed a colorful assault on the island yesterday afternoon by 50 Indians who borrowed a Canadian clipper ship to circle The Rock twice.

Four young braves dived off the barque Monte Cristo and swam to shore during that assault, but were taken back off again by a friendly yachtsman after a caretaker threatened to summon United States marshals.

The Chronicle learned last night, however, that 14 young Indians borrowed another boat and landed on the island undetected. The invading group — which included four girls — carried sleeping bags and food to the island with them.

A proclamation issued by the redmen offered to buy the old Federal prison for "$24 in glass beads and red cloth, a precedent set by the white man's purchase of a similar island 300 years ago.

Seventy-five Indians originally had intended to land on the island yesterday morning in an armada of five borrowed pleasure boats.

But the little fleet failed to show up, so the Indians made a quick bargain with Ronald

Craig, 37, of Vancouver, the owner-captain of the 138-foot barque Monte Cristo.

Craig, who said he agreed to lend his $500,000 ship "because we sympathize with the underdog," even fired a few blank rounds from the vessel's cannons to lend authenticity as the warwhooping Indians circled the island.

Craig kept his passengers about 100 yards offshore, however. Although four or five stalwarts who jumped from the ship made it to shore and briefly claimed the island, it appeared that the Indians would have to settle for less than complete victory.

Indian spokesmen declined

See Back Page

Figure 55 Article by Tim Findley, San Francisco Examiner

Let's Invade Alcatraz

the deck and quarters below."

Jeff added, "We absolutely had no idea anyone had planned on jumping overboard. When I saw the first one jump I did my best to stop them. They put themselves in great danger with the currents."

A Coast Guard officer had boarded the *Monte Cristo* during that exchange. He heard Jeff's explanation. The officer motioned to the agent for a private talk. He whispered to the agent, "He's right. I saw him trying to stop the jumpers."

The agent's return whisper was hoarse and loud enough for others to hear. "I don't care what they say. This damn ship had to be here to help the Indians! They're Canadian. I want you to make sure they leave and they better not commit any infractions! I want you to report to me every day until they leave our waters."

The officer nodded, then, as the agent stomped away, he moved over to face Ron and Jeff. Writing down their names and relationship to the vessel, the officer told them in crisp terms that the *Monte Cristo* was to leave at the earliest opportunity.

Ron nodded agreement. "Yes, I see we have inadvertently upset the agent. We will make preparations to leave. May I ask that we be given a week to resupply and to…"

Jeff had to add, "And to effect repairs to our rigging. Capt. Ip Riis, master of *Balclutha*, docked over there…" Jeff pointed to the far side of the Pier, "very kindly made a list of issues he saw with our lines and stays. It was his opinion that many of those were important safety issues that needed to be corrected before we set sail on the Pacific."

The Coast Guard officer looked up at the rigging. "Lord knows how anyone can find their way through that maze and I am thankful we, on modern ships, don't have to put ourselves through that torture." He shook his head. "Anyway. The *Monte Cristo* is put on notice. Without undue delay, I want you out of port. You have four days."

Four days was more than Ron had hoped for. He and Jeff planned what was needed to be done. The crew who were not delegated to do the repairs or stow the delivered supplies, were on tourist duty. Their publicity had brought long lineups to pay for the privilege of being on the ship that had helped invade Alcatraz.

San Francisco was to have one more surprise for the *Monte Cristo*.

It Had To Be

Rather than being in the way of the crew doing repairs, Ron found he was best suited to lead the tours of visitors. One of the many curious locals brought to Pier 39 was the Australian Consul General with his children. Ron, in full regalia, took charge of this dignified guest. While being shown the fine woodwork on deck, the Consul General happened to mention that Australia was about to stage a massive bicentenary celebration of British explorer James Cook's 200th Anniversary of the discovery of eastern Australia. There would be a re-enactment of the landing in front of the Queen and many heads of state. It would be quite an affair.

A shudder that came from just above them momentarily took their attention. While grown-ups saw nothing, the children stared up at a vision that made them smile.

The Consul General continued, with some regret, explaining that a barquentine, the *Regina Maris*, had been hired to stand in for the *Endeavour* as a last minute substitution for a real barque, "As this is."

The Australian looked pointedly around the three-masted ship. "I don't suppose the *Monte Cristo* would be able to sail the Pacific in time for our little celebration this April?"

> Standing on the main royal yard, the visage of Captain Cook might have been seen by the children rubbing his hands in glee.

Ron jumped right in. "Of course! That would tie in perfectly with our plans!" He turned to Jeff, encouraging agreement.

Jeff had a very peculiar expression. "Ah, actually..."

Ron nodded, "Good! It's settled then."

The Consul General had to slow the pace down. "Well, ah, I was only musing… All right. Allow me to contact Canberra. I promise I will propose this to them. Please give me a few days and, if the plan is accepted, I will invite you to our Consulate to sign the agreement."

> The children looking up gave a delighted squeal and quick applause at the vision of Captain Cook dancing along the yard then twirling into a glittering puff of disappearance.

The day before the Consul General visited, and without any clue whatsoever of the existence of the Australian, Ron had, in some desperation, made a decision. He had handed Jeff $200 with instructions to purchase charts to Panama and into the Caribbean for at least as far as Jamaica.

Jeff later said that he had no idea what possessed him that day. In a bit of a daze, Jeff had set off to buy the Caribbean charts as instructed. Carrying back his newly purchased charts, he realized in astonishment that what he was carrying was an armload of basic charts for the *Pacific*, out to Australia! With that realization, he stood on the sidewalk literally gobsmacked. Confusion rattled around his mind.

His only rational explanation was to remember the time last year, between his initially shipping out on the *Monte Cristo* and later becoming skipper. Jeff was working on a dockside project called the *Explorer*:

> In Bremerton, Washington, I had experienced the inexplicable.
>
> I had heard from the daughter of the *Explorer*'s owner that there was a fortune-teller in Bremerton who supposedly possessed amazing powers. I am not by nature a mystical or philosophical person and am certainly not superstitious, other than following the established seagoing customs of never, if possible, sailing on Fridays, always putting a gold piece under a mast before it is

stepped, and never whistling up a wind. These rituals are kept more as tradition than from fear of consequences if defaulted.

Cheryl, the owner's daughter, convinced me that I might like having a reading from *Myrt*, the seer...

Myrt invited me in and asked if I would like a cup of coffee. As soon as she said that, she corrected herself.

"Oh yes, you drink tea, don't you," she stated.

She returned presently with the cups on a tray and told me, "You're a sailor, but not the type we have around here. You're a real sailor. One who sails sailing ships."

I replied that I was not sailing on any sailing ship at the moment, but wanted to someday.

"You will, within two months," she predicted. "You are going on a long trip," she said.

Here we go, I thought. The next thing she will tell me is that I will meet a dark stranger who will make me wealthy. That should be in the script. I asked her to expand on this. I admitted that a ship I was interested in was planning to sail to the Caribbean to charter there.

"No, it's not going to the Caribbean. You are going to take her to Australia."

Australia? Nobody had mentioned Australia to me before.

"You'll be greeted by thousands of people including heads of state and royalty," Myrt predicted. "You'll have difficult times,

Figure 56 Myrt - from a sketch by Loreena M. Lee

naturally, but everything will be all right in the end."

I thought the prediction about heads of state and royalty a bit over the top, but it made a great way to spend the afternoon. If nothing else, I was getting my money's worth...

I thanked Myrt and said that maybe I would see her again.

No, she told me. She had intimations of her own mortality...

She died shortly after that. And her predictions about me were eerily correct, for reasons I cannot explain.

Perhaps Myrt had been instructed by Captain Cook.

Indeed, the mysterious appearance of the Pacific charts were to become very useful.

Figure 57 Skipper Jeff

The Coast Guard Doesn't Like Us

With preparations having been completed for departure, Ron Craig and Jeff Berry had a final talk before the *Monte Cristo* was to set sail away from San Francisco harbour.

"I've confirmed arrangements for your stay in Monterey. Their own Bicentenary celebrations are running from December through January. 1970 seems to have been a popular time to found places. I showed you the agreement-in-principle from the Australian Consul General." Jeff nodded. "He asked that we keep that under our hat until they work out a gentle way of letting down the owner of the *Regina Maris*."

"She is only a brigantine."

"Which is why the *Monte Cristo* has been promoted by my friend the Consul General as being a more fitting vessel to stand in for Captain Cook's *Endeavour*. At some point, perhaps by the time you get to Tahiti, we'll have official confirmation."

Jeff added, "And we will need to change her name to *Endeavour II*."

Ron paused. "Oh. Of course. You'll need to tell me what that process entails…"

"Ship's registry details – I can list the steps for you – and a new nameplate for the bow…"

On writing those new notes, Ron had noticed an expense entry written by Jeff. "It cost *how much* to load the ship with another ten tons of ballast? What is this shot material?"

Jeff explained patiently that the *Monte Cristo* could not be safely sailed on the Pacific without the extra steel punchings as ballast. It was arranged into a series of wooden boxes built under the Saloon and engine room. The balancing of the ship with her new ballast was directed by Captain Riis. Under his watchful eye, the ten tons was guided into the correct boxes so that the ship floated true in the water. "A *further* ten tons will be needed, Jeff. As is, this ship is sitting precariously on a bubble. You will have your hands full keeping her in trim," Riis had warned.

Ron's notebook was filling up with Jeff's extensive details of supplies needed and things to do, along with an ever-growing contact list at ports-of-call, and with names of potential crew members who needed interviewing.

At the previous late night meeting, Ron pointed to his list of current candidates. "What do you think of these dozen names, Jeff?"

Jeff scowled, "I read their letters. So many young people these days cannot write a coherent sentence. In any case, the crew we decide on, as well as the four still with us, will need to go through a rigorous training program. I was embarrassed by the comments that Captain Riis had regarding our shoddy seamanship. And that was before we even set a sail. I promise that we will leave under the Golden Gate Bridge in better shape than when we arrived." Nodding at two underlined names in Ron's notebook, "If those two, especially, sign on at Monterey, by then we may truly be considered to have a passable crew."

Ron nodded in sync with the visage of Captain Cook, shimmering on the cabin wall.

"Exactly what I want to hear, Jeff. Oh, by the way. Tell me what time you expect to be leaving. The Coast Guard has been threatening to

The Coast Guard Doesn't Like Us

serve papers if we are not shipped out by noon the latest. They really don't like us anymore."

The *Monte Cristo* left San Francisco harbour before midday. A Coast Guard ship not only followed them past the Golden Gate Bridge, it accompanied them for at least an hour as they motored out along the shipping channel then bore south. Jeff raised them on the shortwave as they dropped behind then turned away from the *Monte Cristo*. It was a friendly goodbye on Jeff's part. He had expected a "fair winds" from the Coast Guard captain but their only response was a gruff reminder that the *Monte Cristo* was under watch.

Taking advantage of good weather, Jeff carried on with his crew training. With increasing eagerness, most of the crew participated in classes on basic seamanship, nomenclature, ship maintenance, and the many tasks needed to be done automatically when the master issued sailing instructions.

They went over such arcane things as what is an *evolution* and how does one handle the peak halyards during an evolution. For the crew members still on board, these details were part of why they signed on. A real high-mast seaman could be distinguished from a crew member of a tramp steamer. They were the rough-and-ready elite of the sailing world.

Making into Monterey just prior to Christmas, the *Monte Cristo* docked, as Ron had arranged, in a prominent location for the city's Bicentenary celebrations. There was little rest for the crew, however. While there, a new diesel engine was installed – a GMC 6-71 developing two hundred and fifty horsepower. It had a more aggressive propeller and shaft to match the output. The next requirement Jeff told Ron to write into his to-do list was a suitable engine control system. The current system was woefully inadequate. They did make sure that there was a shut off valve on the exhaust pipe, to avoid another flooded engine.

As promised back in San Francisco, Ron was pleased to sign on a twenty-nine year-old Chief Mate by the name of Mike Jefferies. Their new mate's sailing experience had been on schooners which were *gaff-rigged*. Those boat's sails are not square – rather they are trapezoidal, with a standard lower boom, but with the upper part of the canvas held out further than a triangular sail can reach, by a pole, or "gaff". Mike was familiar, therefore, with the aft *spanker* sail on the *Monte Cristo*, as it was gaff-rigged. He had some learning to do for the rest of the square-rigged ship. Mike had been trained very well by an experienced sailor named Captain Omar Darr, as well as having learned rigging from an authentic old salt, Jack Dickerhoff, which impressed and gratified Jeff.

The new bosun was an acquaintance of Mike's. Lauren (Larry) Williams also had solid sailing experience. Other seamen were signed on there or were to come aboard further down the coast. The abilities of the new crew put real confidence in Ron's mind. He forged ahead with his plans to raise money to further equip the *Monte Cristo,* to chase her destiny across the Pacific.

Still docked at Monterey, the new diesel had needed a new bed to secure it. Showing right away his innate desire to work hard, Larry took charge of that task. It was dirty work, packing concrete into voids under the engine. The wet, dark, cramped area had oily bilge water sloshing around it. A worn old electrical cord from Larry's work-light was dangling just above the water. Jeff and Mike were crouched above Larry, handing down buckets of concrete and encouragement as needed.

Mike reached over for another bucket when Jeff noticed Larry jerking wildly. "What the…? LARRY! Quick Mike! Haul him up!"

The cord had dipped into the water and it was electrocuting Larry! Instinctively, they each grabbed one of Larry legs and yanked him up; even in that instant they felt the electricity jolt through their wet hands. The momentum flung Larry over their heads and sent him tumbling into the Saloon. He sprawled out, panting shallowly on the deck.

Still teetering near the opening, Jeff looked over his shoulder and was relieved to see Larry's panting.

Shaking with the exertion, Mike scrambled to the shaking bosun. "Larry! Jesus! You alright?"

At the same time Jeff found himself holding onto a section of the cord. The instant he noticed it, Jeff flung it away as if it were a poisonous snake.

Larry had been badly stunned. When he finally found control of his voice, it was at a higher pitch. "I'm, I'm going to have to take the rest of the day off. If that's OK with you, Skipper?"

"Fine! Of course! Are you sure you're not hurt?"

Larry rolled over to get up. As he did so, his one leg nearly gave way but he persevered by holding onto a chair. Collecting himself resolutely, he spoke through clenched teeth, "Just another day at the office."

Two days later, Larry forced himself to show up. To any question about his swollen, limping leg, Larry answered tersely, "Sprained."

Larry limped on from job to job. There had been much to do, starting with renewing the spanker gaff jaws, which had been smashed when one of the crew had incorrectly let go of the peak halyards (the line that raises the further end of the sail) during an evolution. He also decided to

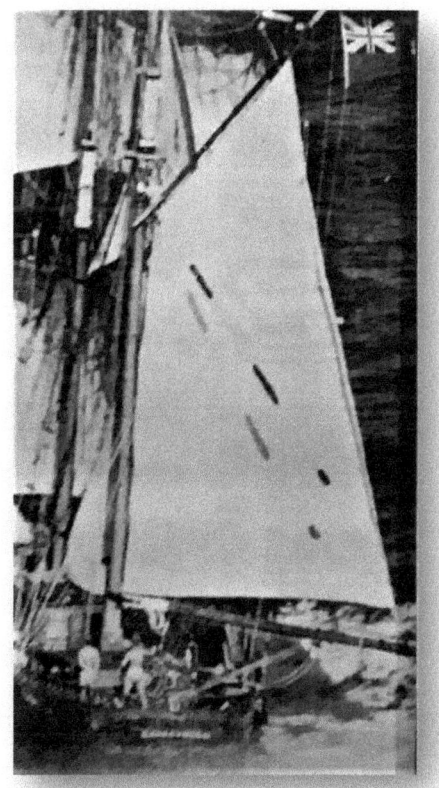

Figure 58 Larry's new spanker sail

recut the spanker sail, deleting one complete cloth from the leech (trailing edge). This allowed it to set tightly and take a useful shape.

Working her way down the California coast, Ron stayed several jumps ahead arranging for the *Monte Cristo* to be viewed, for a small fee, at marinas and community functions.

One of the more hazardous excursions they had was to Santa Catalina Island where Jeff and Mike were tasked nearly to the breaking point as they had to pick their way around the myriad moorings of very expensive yachts.

The US Coast Guard's opinion of the *Monte Cristo* was not improved when the ship inadvertently dragged her anchor, fouling it with those of the aforementioned expensive yachts.

In Newport Beach, the anchor ruckus caused more Coast Guard inspectors to visit, what they now branded, the Canadian "klutz" ship.

Perhaps it was inevitable – with the officers and crew of the sailing ship still in training – that one of the Coast Guard captains in San Diego HQ had it in his mind that the *Monte Cristo* must be doing something nefarious. At the very least, he suspected them of taking money illegally for day cruises or for passage on a longer voyage on the Pacific.

Jeff's entreaties to the Coast Guard captain had not been well received. "Sir, we well know the provisions of the Jones Act. The only fees we have received were while docked, and only for visitors to tour the vessel at that time. When you say that the owner, Mr. Craig, was speaking with people about sailing to Australia, I can guarantee that he was looking for regular crew members, only. We absolutely will not be selling berths on our vessel while in American waters. And, I take full responsibility for any upset I caused when our anchor fouled on those of the yachts. As you can plainly see from my papers, this is my first command of a barque."

The inspecting captain was not persuaded. In his most officious manner, he berated Master Jeff Berry. "While in my waters you've caused me no end of trouble. The reports I had from respectable and experienced sailors off Santa Catalina were that the *Monte Cristo* harboured, to put it mildly, a rag-tag crew who blundered about carelessly among the vessels of respectable yachtsmen. And, as sure as the sun will rise in the morn, I am certain you have come here in a blatant effort to make money at the expense of innocent Americans. How, I will uncover in due time."

While the captain had Jeff's attention, his inspectors were harassing the prospective crew members, trying to get them to admit that Ron Craig had offered them a berth in exchange for cash. Since that had not been the case with these sailors, the inspectors found nothing wrong.

Later that day, a phone call was made to the docked ship. It was from a Coast Guard chief petty officer – CPO – who had been upset at his boss' haranguing of Ron and Jeff. The CPO told them to "watch out for Wally. He's the captain's nephew. He's going to try giving you money to sail with you to Australia."

Half an hour after the phone call, a prospective seaman called Wally walked up the gangway.

As soon as Wally started into his patter, Ron and Jeff exchanged winks. Wally was about to bring out a cash payment to "become a crewman".

Jeff kept his hands in his pockets. "Wally, I have to inform you that you are breaking the provisions of the United States Jones Act. The penalty for such an infraction is a fine of $10,000 and five years in jail. I must inform you that on offering us money, you are in violation of the Federal Statute and we are obliged to advise the authorities forthwith. Just to keep Canadian-American relations amicable, you know."

With his jaw dropping, Wally spun on his heels and took off faster than a scalded cat. As he passed Larry on the gangway he moaned, "Unc didn't tell me this was going to happen!"

Hard Lessons at San Diego

On the way from San Francisco, Jeff had his hands full showing the still skeleton crew what they needed to do, even while motoring. The few sails they were able to set with this crew served to confirm a number of deficiencies in the *Monte Cristo*'s rigging. Jeff made mental notes to add to those that Captain Riis gave in San Francisco.

A thorny issue that Jeff had to deal with resulted from his young age and his preference to maintain a professional attitude. Most sailors were ready to *let go* at the drop of a hat. Jeff always stayed in control. This caused a few of the experienced seamen to push back when Jeff gave instructions. From his US Navy experience, Jeff did not expect it and wasn't certain how to handle such insolence. He just put up with it.

Prior to the *Monte Cristo* reaching San Diego, Ron, on shore, had been able to sift through the many names of seamen who had wanted to sign on. It was to be a hectic time at their final dock in US waters, with repairs to the rigging, training of seamen in the peculiarities of the *Monte Cristo*, and training a new engineer.

Ron made a point of noting to Jeff that Dorothy Smith, Ron's wife, would be greatly missed. She had said she would be leaving the ship in San Diego. "Dorothy is the hardest working hand aboard."

She would be returning to her home in Lynden, Washington.

Their destination in San Diego was Harbor Island. This was a favourite location for yachtsmen. Moorage was usually at a premium, since so many locals and visitors gathered at the island's facilities, protected as they were from the open sea.

It was a few days before Christmas, 1969, as the *Monte Cristo* made a cautious approach to Marina Cortez. Ron had made his usual arrangements, finding a prominent berth where the visiting public would best see the grand ship.

One of the new crew, Bantam Smith, asked for permission to leave for Christmas. It was not easy to give permission. Even with a skeleton crew, they were under pressure to carry on with repairs. Jeff's list included replacing the remaining manila rope with nylon, greasing the deadeyes with tallow, and greeting the paying visitors.

On Christmas Day there were several guests who were treated by Ron to a large dinner. The event also served to welcome the new crew.

No rest for the next day, as rotted woodwork was replaced at the forecastle, and 80 gallons of propane was brought on board for cooking. Later they were to find a leaking tank which needed to be replaced.

Captain Berry was invited to the USS *Fresno* (LST 1182) for dinner. The Navy ship had been commissioned just a month previously and was homeported in San Diego. It was common courtesy for Navy captains to invite current or former Naval officers, as Jeff was, aboard.

The log of the *Monte Cristo* noted that, on December 26th seaman John Dye was a.w.o.l. He was recorded as returning the next day. Later, Jeff and the new Mate, Mike Jefferies, discussed their crew discipline issue. Mike was one of the seamen who were, basically, jealous of Jeff's position, so the relationship was occasionally a bit strained.

"Mike, I am not comfortable with your allowing John back aboard with no punishment. I wouldn't recommend anything more than a severe talking-to, but we should have done that, at least. He was needed for the line replacement work."

Hard Lessons at San Diego

"Now, Jeff. He's just a young man, homesick at Christmas. This isn't a Navy ship, after all."

"Not Navy, by any means, but when we finally set sail for Tahiti, it will be a rough and dangerous passage. The crew must be used to discipline or someone will get hurt."

Mike was not convinced, though he had to agree that this was not going to be a pleasure trip.

Entries in the log for subsequent days showed that the crew went through sail drills, repaired a newly discovered design flaw in the topgallant trestle truss, and they welcomed aboard a well-known shipwright, Drake Thomas, for an extended tour of the vessel.

New Year's Day was to be one of Ron's high publicity days. He had advertised the *Monte Cristo* extensively in the local paper and with posters, promising they would, "Ring in the New Year with a Blast!"

During the couple days' absence of Captain Berry to the Navy ship, Mate Jefferies oversaw the aforesaid blast. He had coached John Springer on loading and firing one of their token deck cannon with black powder charges. The amount of the powder was calculated to make a sufficient din accompanied by lots of smoke. Of course, nobody would be hurt because it was only loaded with newspaper.

A large crowd had gathered to witness the New Year's event.

Springer performed well with the first charge, creating excitement in the gathered crowd watching from onshore. In a hurry to set off the next charge, he forgot Jefferies' instructions and rammed the second charge into the still-hot barrel. He was supposed to swab the barrel first, to cool it down. The hot barrel caused the second charge to flash, blowing Springer to the deck. His right hand suffered powder burns and he was taken quickly to the Community Hospital.

Shortly after that excitement, another new seaman, Maxfield Smith reported aboard.

Captain Berry returned the next day. He was greeted by an upset Ron Craig.

"I don't know what's going on here, Jeff. You leave for a couple days and all hell breaks loose! I don't want the *Monte Cristo Cruise Line* to go back to the mess we had with Gilchrist!"

"I heard about the injury to Springer. When I saw him in the hospital they said he would be there a few days but he should be fine to ship out with us. Did the last supply delivery arrive?"

Ron rolled his eyes. "More expense. And, yes, I approved the electrician work to rewire the engine room, and the carpenter from Nelson's Boatyard to build the icebox, and the pipefitter to finish the Galley's propane piping, and more nylon and cable and…"

"Sir, these are all absolutely necessary, as you know. Captain Riis went over the list…"

"Yes, yes. I know. Now. If I had known how much it would cost to sail to Australia I might… Anyway, negotiations are progressing well with the Australians. I still expect to have final approval by the time you reach Tahiti."

In the midst of their work it was necessary to move the ship more than once. The marina needed them out of the way for the higher value day-trippers.

They still had not installed a usable engine control system. The new engineer's training included a cumbersome routine to inform him of the skipper's orders.

To add to Jeff's concerns, Ron was on the dock at the time, in costume, ready to welcome visitors at a small table that was set up where the gangplank was to be dropped.

In fine weather, Jeff had been using the cumbersome surplus US Navy sound-powered "telephone" to give instructions down to his rookie engineer. Testing of the process just before the harbour

Hard Lessons at San Diego

approach was successful. The cramped engine room forced the engineer into some ambidextrous maneuvering, but he responded to orders correctly.

Bringing the *Monte Cristo* into port amongst the many smaller yachts was like directing an elephant, adorned with overhanging displays, through a crowd of show horses whose riders were twirling lassos. The clearance needed to pass each yacht included the beam of the ship, of course, but also the mast stays and overhanging yards of the ship.

In order to obtain a better view of the route through the maze, Jeff climbed up four ratlines of the mizzen rigging. Line handlers were arranged on the portside.

Aiming for the berth he was assigned, Jeff ordered the helmsman to steer a 45 degree angle toward the dock, using what had become a standard approach. Jeff yelled down, "Slow Ahead!" to the engineer.

Although the engineer acknowledged the command, *Monte Cristo*'s new diesel droned on without change. Entering the final approach, and seeing no slow-down, Jeff then commanded "Stop Engine!"

The engineer responded through the phone with, "Stop Engine", but it was still plowing ahead. In the berth ahead of their target was a 30-ft. fiberglass ketch. It would not have been proper to use it as a bumper.

More urgently, Jeff yelled for others on the deck to confirm with the engineer that he was to respond immediately to the orders. There was no change in the engine r.p.m.

Jeff then ordered the helmsman to sheer off.

Sitting on the dock watching with growing horror was Ron Craig. The cash box, brochures and a telephone on the small table in front of him were ignored as the *Monte Cristo* came barreling toward him.

Jeff yelled, "Full Astern!"

With that, the engineer put the engine into idle. The *Monte Cristo* still maintained unwanted forward momentum, careening past the ketch. The large, overhanging main yard caught the ketch's mainmast, snapping its backstays and pulling the rig with sickening snaps and twangs as the wires broke.

They finally stopped. At that point the engineer decided to put the engine into *Full Astern*! That reversal caused the battering ram of a ship to take out the ketch's mizzenmast.

After that last maneuver, all the yelling had finally got the engineer to go to *Full Stop*.

If the event was a movie, perhaps Charlie Chaplin would have starred in it as the engineer. All Jeff and Ron could see, however, was the huge cost and embarrassment. Sitting on the dock next to his ship, Ron's head dropped to the table, shaking back and forth.

> Up on the main royal, Captain Cook's open mouth of disbelief was covered with yet another face-slap.

With angry muttering of strings of mariner's expletives, Jeff had the crew tie up to the dock. It was then that the engineer popped his head out from the engine room, looking for all the world like an innocent ground hog, to see what the excitement had been about. He expressed an instant of shock and then he jumped to the dock and ran off, never to be heard from again.

The skipper and first mate of the *Monte Cristo* sheepishly climbed over to inspect the yacht's damage. They wrote down that the masts and some stays had received the brunt of the attack.

Little on the *Monte Cristo* needed repair from the collision. In the calm after the storm, the dealer who owned the damaged boat provided a list of repair items, totaling $2500. On second and third thoughts, this soon ballooned to $10,000.

Subsequently, Ron negotiated with the ketch owner, who had, in effect, slapped a lien on the ship. Jeff and Mike carefully went over

Hard Lessons at San Diego

the *Monte Cristo's* surface scratches, taking the few days' down-time to deal with further issues in the rigging.

Despite the incident having been caused by the engineer's mistakes, it had to be the skipper who wore the fault. The evening of the collision, Jeff sat through a tongue lashing by Ron.

"Here I am scratching out barely enough to pay costs day-by-day and you run my ship into a land-shark's yacht! How am I supposed to pay his $10,000 bill?"

The only thing that saved Jeff's job was the fact that Ron had been an eye witness to the events and had seen who was at fault.

A substantially lower settlement was arrived at, but it still hurt.

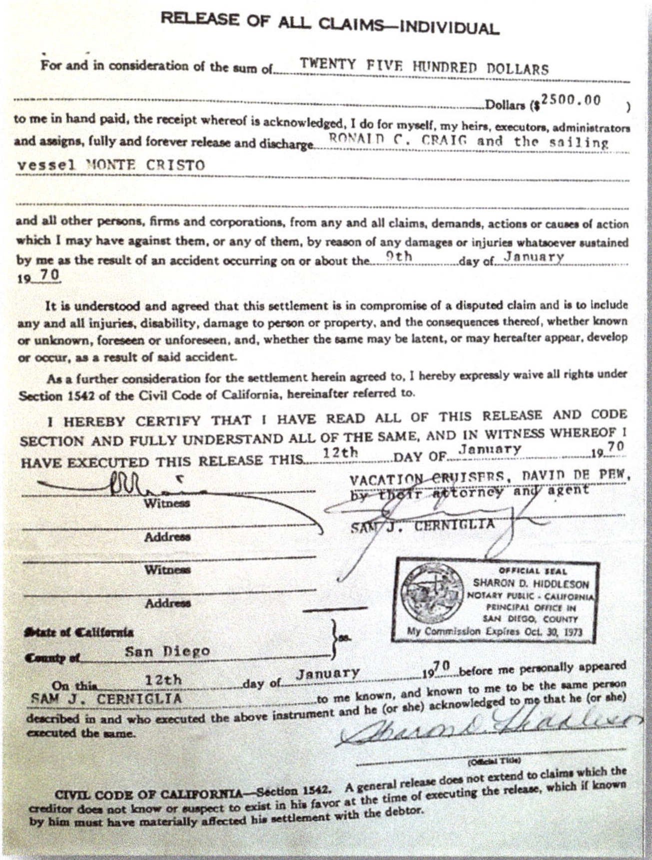

RELEASE OF ALL CLAIMS—INDIVIDUAL

For and in consideration of the sum of TWENTY FIVE HUNDRED DOLLARS Dollars ($2500.00)

to me in hand paid, the receipt whereof is acknowledged, I do for myself, my heirs, executors, administrators and assigns, fully and forever release and discharge RONALD C. CRAIG and the sailing vessel MONTE CRISTO

and all other persons, firms and corporations, from any and all claims, demands, actions or causes of action which I may have against them, or any of them, by reason of any damages or injuries whatsoever sustained by me as the result of an accident occurring on or about the 9th day of January 19 70

It is understood and agreed that this settlement is in compromise of a disputed claim and is to include any and all injuries, disability, damage to person or property, and the consequences thereof, whether known or unknown, foreseen or unforeseen, and, whether the same may be latent, or may hereafter appear, develop or occur, as a result of said accident.

As a further consideration for the settlement herein agreed to, I hereby expressly waive all rights under Section 1542 of the Civil Code of California, hereinafter referred to.

I HEREBY CERTIFY THAT I HAVE READ ALL OF THIS RELEASE AND CODE SECTION AND FULLY UNDERSTAND ALL OF THE SAME, AND IN WITNESS WHEREOF I HAVE EXECUTED THIS RELEASE THIS 12th DAY OF January 1970

Witness
Address
Witness
Address

VACATION CRUISERS, DAVID DE PEW, by their attorney and agent
SAM J. CERNIGLIA

OFFICIAL SEAL
SHARON D. HIDDLESON
NOTARY PUBLIC - CALIFORNIA
PRINCIPAL OFFICE IN
SAN DIEGO COUNTY
My Commission Expires Oct. 30, 1973

State of California }
County of San Diego } ss.

On this 12th day of January 1970 before me personally appeared SAM J. CERNIGLIA to me known, and known to me to be the same person described in and who executed the above instrument and he (or she) acknowledged to me that he (or she) executed the same.

(Official Title)

CIVIL CODE OF CALIFORNIA—Section 1542. A general release does not extend to claims which the creditor does not know or suspect to exist in his favor at the time of executing the release, which if known by him must have materially affected his settlement with the debtor.

Figure 59 Release from further legal action

Details

The *Monte Cristo* had been built, as Captain Cook would say, without a "purpose" in mind. Was it to puddle jump in calm seas from port to nearby port; was it to carry cargo; was it to race the high seas? Making it ready for a run across the Pacific required that the crew of about twenty seamen had places to sleep, eat and entertain themselves. Safety equipment such as life rafts were needed for that number of crew, plus an extra margin. Dry and secure storage areas were needed for the food, water and other supplies.

All these must be completed, along with the needed rigging improvements and structural repairs, before leaving San Diego.

The new crew were kept busy on the ship. Ron was raising money and negotiating with ports enroute, as well telephoning regularly to Australian officials about their part in the Bicentenary Celebrations. Jeff was tending to the logistics of how much of which supplies would be needed, who of the crew was to be doing which tasks, preparing for the daunting work of navigating across the Pacific to successfully hit tiny islands on the other side of the equator – using what we would now call rudimentary tools – and, his least liked task, dealing with personalities. A captain, as James Cook well knew, had to juggle numerous hard problems, but it was the soft problems of personalities that could be the tripper.

Everything being as ready as it could be, January 12, 1970 was set as the day to leave San Diego for Mexican waters. They cleared Customs for Ensenada. A US Marshall came aboard to release the ship of the claims due to damages to that ketch they had used for a bumper. All loose items on deck were lashed or stowed.

The *Monte Cristo* backed out of their slip (successfully). *Slow Ahead* was signaled to the *new* new engineer. Clearing San Diego Bay, they began sea trials for the engine and the new electrical wiring, attaining a top speed of 6.2 knots.

At midnight, Jeff wrote a special entry in the log: "What a hectic day this has been."

Motoring and then giving the crew time to exercise on the sails, they made Ensenada late at night on January 13th.

The ship was in a slip after midnight. Jeff and Mike cleared Customs the next morning, giving most of the crew leave to go ashore.

As of January 15th, two watches were established:

Starboard Watch	Port Watch
Capt. Jeff Berry	*Mate* Michael Jefferies
Lauren (Larry) Williams, *bosun*	John Dye, *seaman*
Ed Adams, *seaman*	John Springer, *seaman*
John Taylor, *seaman*	Stewart Smith, *seaman*
Richard Hite, *seaman*	Sam Bukema, *Cabin Boy*
Phillip Groce, doctor, *seaman*	Douglas DuMaurier, *seaman*
John Steers, *seaman*	Richard Caster, *seaman*
Bruce Doorly, *seaman*	Maureen Higgins, *nurse, seaman*
Kathy Kelly, *seaman*	Marsha Ross, *seaman*
Brian Hard, *engineer*	Dennis and Linda Praigg, *cooks*

Each of the crew had a story. Mike had brought the cabin boy. Larry Williams was the lone Canadian left on the crew. The token Australian was the engineer, Brian Hard. John Springer had just left the US Air Force (intelligence and translation, listening to Czech Air Force radio). Richard Hite wore a flamboyant Bowie knife in a tooled leather

Details

sheath on his belt. The sheath read "Puma Killer", so that was his moniker. The final experienced seaman on the crew was John Taylor.

In Mexican waters (not in US waters), they also signed on John Steers, John Dye, Richard Caster and Douglas Du Maurier. None of these eager volunteers had sailed the deep sea before. However, they had kicked in several thousands each to offset the costs of making the trip.

> Captain Cook looked down from a high yard at the untested crew.
>
> *"It is good to be underway. It is not good to have that mix of potential emotional turmoil, both mercenary sailors and women. Seamen not fully committed to the ship are a thorn in everyone's side. And we have not been comfortable with such a number of women on a sailing vessel, not because they are women; but because there are men."*

Before Mexican authorities would allow them to leave their jurisdiction, a substantial bribe was needed. Aside from standard procedure, a further extra amount was quietly expected to offset actions of their California nemesis, the righteously indignant US Coast Guard captain. When his continuing inquiries confirmed that crewmen did pay to sail on the *Monte Cristo*, even if it was in Mexico, he pulled all the cross-border strings he could.

Several hundred greenbacks served to release the ship.

On January 16th, the *Monte Cristo* was cleared for Tahiti.

They very quickly realized something: the Pacific is one big ocean.

Details

Facts About Sailing the Pacific

It is really hard.

Out of the bay area of Ensenada, the *Monte Cristo* passed Islas de Todos Santo, steering 215°. Eighteen hours out, it was abundantly plain that they were on the deep sea.

As Jeff and Mike continued finding and ordering repairs to the rigging, reality set in to most of the crew. Trade winds were blowing to the southwest with steady ten to twelve knots of breeze. The *Monte Cristo* was up to her old habit of hobby-horsing. The pitching combined with the deep sea swells caused some of the new seamen to turn a sickly yellow/green.

Figure 60 On the Pacific

Facts About Sailing the Pacific

Out of the blue, two of the new crew suddenly remembered that they had important business ashore, so could the captain please reverse course and head back to Mexico?

Not at all pleased with their request, Jeff held his temper. "Lads, this is not a cruise ship that you signed on for. If you have a legitimate medical emergency, Dr. Phil Groce must make that call. Besides, from what I've seen before, even the worst seasickness usually cures itself within three days, or sooner. When you join a sailing ship you join a part of the real world of hard knocks. You are not permitted to cut and run if the going gets a little tougher than you imagined."

He ordered them to lay aloft and furl the royal sails. The wind was gusting at the time so Jeff wanted to ease his new crew into the difficult tasks one step at a time. They lowered the yards, secured the braces then clewed up the sails before furling. The reluctant sailors hesitantly climbed the ratlines, clinging amateurly to the shrouds as they ascended.

The royal yard was the highest square sail that *Monte Cristo* set. That sail was whipping around in its slings and needed to be rough-furled at the least, otherwise it would be torn. Time was of the essence, as Jeff yelled up to them. The men got as far as the topgallant yard level, stared up at the royal, which was by now barely under control from the buntlines and clew lines.

Jeff could see them chattering back and forth to each other as they held very tightly to the shroud. One was being quite emphatic with a free hand, making negative gestures up at the rigging and down at the deck.

Thinking they saw some sort of rigging foul, Jeff bellowed up, "What's the problem?"

They didn't reply as they climbed back down to the deck.

"How much does that sail cost?" the animated one asked.

"About eight-hundred dollars. What's the problem up there?"

Facts About Sailing the Pacific

At that, the sailor slipped down the booby hatch into the forecastle. He returned with a wad of his Travelers cheques.

"Here," he said to Jeff. "This is for the sail. Can't go up there again. If she shreds, this'll pay for it."

The skipper could see that he had to teach them, more or less respectfully, how to become seamen. Jeff refused the payment. "Besides, we have no replacement canvas aboard!"

To encourage the two volunteer sailors to get moving, Jeff reluctantly broke out his prolific vocabulary of mariner's lingo, tongue lashing them into submission.

Heads lowered, both of them sheepishly succumbed. They laid aloft, and, encouraging each other, they actually went all the way out onto the royal yard. In a few minutes they had the sail under control.

It took a short time before both men were able to do this with confidence.

The vastness of the water, everywhere, all around their little ship, brought home to the crew that no problem was *little*. Everything had to work now, or else.

The creaks appeared to grow louder. Stays appeared looser.

When water in the bilge was found, anxious seamen checked it regularly.

Jeff and Mike concluded that the excess may have come from poor seals around the port lights.

A rum ration was issued on the first day at sea at 1400 hours. For those who have not been to sea by sail, which included most of the crew other than Jeff, Mike and a couple others, the relaxing value of the rum ration was brought home after its effect seeped in.

For Jeff and Mike, into whose hands the crew placed their trust, the responsibility of keeping the crews' hands and minds occupied became an on-going chore.

The weather started out quite pleasant, so, on the 19th, they *goose-winged* the mainsail – meaning that the mainsail and adjoining staysail where both raised side-by-side so as to capture as much wind as they could, without having to use the upper or forward sails. This helped in reducing the ship's hobby-horsing tendencies but required the helmsman to keep a close eye on changing wind direction. Their average speed in that configuration was a respectable 6 knots.

A hand-powered bilge pump was installed to clear the bilge.

The crew were employed in making baggywrinkle, which is soft cloth sections placed in locations where the canvas of the sails would otherwise chafe against hard surfaces. They made jib sheet pendants, overhauled the main topgallant and royal running gear, and cleared the bilge again. And again.

One may, rightly, become anal about clearing the bilge on a wooden vessel in the middle of the Pacific. The log started to take on a repetitiveness that explained what was important:

> **Jan. 21**: sunrise at 0630; sighted American Export Lines C-3 freighter – no communication received; bilge pumped with 205 strokes via main pump; sail drill; lit diesel to charge batteries for 1 hr.; average speed 4.5 knots; noon position L23° 41.0N, λ120° 19.5W; 110 mi. run.
>
> **Jan. 22**: sail drill; main bilge 170 strokes; deck washdown; at 1400 served beer ration; sunset at 1750; charged batteries; average speed 5.2 knots; 130 miles run.
>
> **Jan 23**: sunrise at 0630; washdown; bilge pump 96 strokes; sail drill; on starting engine for battery recharge, engineer failed to open exhaust valve and filled lower deck with smoke; exhausted by opening forecastle escape hatch; average speed 5 knots, 121 miles.
>
> **Jan 24**: routine; sunset at 1755; Victory ship crossed ½ cable away

but attempts to signal unsuccessful; avg. speed 5.7 kt, 113 mi.

Jan 25: 0045, attempt to tack but missed stays; 0630 sunrise; 1400 rum ration; avg speed 7 kt; 174 mi.

Jan 26: 0620 sunrise; bilge 225 strokes at 0630, again 225 at 1545; sunset at 1825; avg 602 kt; 148 mi...

A sailor was once asked, after making the short crossing of the Salish Sea from Vancouver to Nanaimo, "How was the crossing?"

The questioner, a non-sailor, was expecting a fascinating tale of nearly hitting a pod of Orcas, having the bow raised by a breaching Grey Whale, avoiding deep-running nuclear subs, and being pounded by inclement weather.

Instead, the sailor politely said, "First there was a wave, and then another one, and another one, and one more, and then the same thing happened again."

While there can be excitement on the open ocean, it more often resembles the description of flying a small plane: 95% boring routine punctuated by 5% sheer terror.

Figure 61 Below deck

At the same time, one would think that a seaman would have plenty of time to catch up on those books that were never finished: *War and Peace; Pride and Prejudice; Macbeth...*

Indeed many new sailors embarking on a long voyage pack those books, envisioning long, sunny afternoons lounging on the deck, reading to their heart's content. Very few of the bags containing such books are ever unpacked during a sailing excursion. It is not that there may be some downtime – moments may be found between watches. External considerations usually interfere with what may be intended as a period of cerebral cogitation. Things like the incessant salty spray, a constantly rolling deck, pranks from fellow crew, calls for "All hands aloft" in a rising gale, and just plain ennui.

Even an engaging book may not be completed between Mexico and French Polynesia. Others matters arise to occupy one's mind.

What humans do to allay a boring life is, too often, to form groups and then verbally assault nearby groups. Thus, the smallest incident on board a ship would become a reason to associate with a support group, then to mount a (usually) verbal attack on an individual. The attackee would, of necessity, seek solace in another group, and so the battle lines are drawn.

Normally, it is the job of a ship's captain and his mate to nip such preoccupations in the bud. However, when one of the groups is fomented by the mate, in opposition to the captain, the situation becomes problematic, as the real story of Captain Blye will attest to.

Still, the ship sailed on:

> **Jan 30:** night watch; set and took in main sail several times due to squalls; bilge 300 strokes; sunrise at 0615; switched to #3 propane tank - #2 lasted 11 days; struck by severe southerly squall – scrambled to take in sails; deficiencies found in main and main topgallant, leechline blocks; avg 4.1 kt; 48 mi.
>
> **Jan 31:** 0100 motor vessel passed across bow 200 yd, turned their searchlight on; identity of vessel unknown; did not answer our hail; 0315 doldrums, so lit engine; 1340 set some sail; avg 2.1 kt; 51 mi, 32 powered.
>
> **Feb 1:** secured running lights at 0620; bilge 245 strokes; rope jammed; no work done this Sabbath; prep to launch small boat; launched at 1500; Mate Michael and Phil in boat to take pictures; sunset at 1900; avg speed 5.2 kt; 110 mi by sail, 13 mi powered;

total passage 1903 mi.

Feb 2: Secured running lights at 0630; 194 bilge; avg speed 5.3 kt; rhumbline distance to Nuku Hiva 1010 mi.

Feb 3: sunrise at 0646; bilge 165 strokes; retarded clocks for time zone +9 V; received CBC shortwave broadcast; avg speed 5.2 kt; 124 mi; total 2156 mi.

Feb 4: at 0200 crossed Equator at λ129° 58W by dead reckoning; secured lights at 0530; bilge 184; Neptune Rep traditional line-crossing ceremony at 1400; avg speed 5.17 kt.

Crossing the Equator was, and continues today, to be time for a special ceremony. At its simplest, those who have not yet crossed that widest part of the Earth are termed *polliwogs*, or *wogs*. Those who have done so once are *shellbacks*. In the model of a hazing

Figure 62 from "Captain Cook" map, http://www.history-map.com/

ceremony, the mariner who has crossed most often takes on the role of Neptune, who, with his retinue of old hands, subjects the wogs to certain secret, often vile, tests. One less objectional test is to kiss a particularly ugly fish on the lips.

> The actions we take upon one another when we hold power over them! It is good to maintain traditions. It is not good to fall into brutality for the sake of personal power. The greater the power we may have, the stronger must be our conscience and sense of morality to counter the basest consequences of unbridled power.

On February 9th, the Marquesas Islands were sighted. Hitting French Polynesia so accurately after more than 3000 miles of sailing was, perhaps, the only good news Jeff had. Pride in his navigation abilities was short-lived.

The mood amongst the crew was dreadful.

Back-biting, accusations, demands, and general emotional turmoil were increasing the closer they sailed to Tahiti. From the Marquesas to Tahiti, it was as if a contagion hit them.

Within sight of paradise, half the crew had developed a vague desire to mutiny. Their courage to do so, fortunately for the safety of the ship, did not resolve into action until they arrived at Papeete.

What To Do In Tahiti

The crew's mood was not improved as they sailed into the Marquesas Islands on their way to Tahiti.

Sailors termed the Marquesas Islands the gates of Hades, through which one had to pass in order to make it to Paradise.

The islands harboured cannibals until 1926.

They were the storm-tossed seas of *Moby Dick*, as Herman Melville had described it after he deserted his whaling ship to hide near the cannibals on Nuku Hiva.

Active, cloud-spewing volcanoes formed most of what jutted up through the ocean surface. This group of islands is the furthest one can be from any continental shore.

While docked for five days at Taioha'e Bay, Nuku Hiva, those who had retained their initiative assisted in repairs. They worked on projects such as the fabrication of the spanker throat halyard stop. During this repair, Bruce Dooley was injured in the face by a come-along. He was taken to hospital for stitching. In later years, his wounds were worn proudly.

Water was painstakingly brought aboard one jerry-can at a time. If on shore leave, the crew went off to view the cascade waterfall, or attend a party given by the French Army doctor, whose household were overjoyed to see these *European* visitors. Jeff went on an eventful horse-ride. The mare was trained in French and would not take commands in English. With much cursing of the French he knew, he rode to Typee Valley to see the ruins of ancient stonework. On turning back, the mare would take orders in no language at all, screamed or not, as it galloped at full speed back to its stall at the bottom of the mountain. It was a good thing Jeff had ridden lively horses in the past.

Talk on board by one group centred around the idea of reaching Tahiti as if it were to be an emergence from their perceived torture on board the *Monte Cristo*. Looking forward to putting the Marquesas Islands to their stern, some of the crew privately voiced the sacrilegious: they were going to quit this damn ship and bask in Paradise!

How many sailors have succumbed to that siren call in these seas?

Having left for Rangiroa Atoll on February 14th, the *Monte Cristo* maneuvered carefully through dangerous waters for over 570 miles.

> **Feb 15**: On course to Takaroa; dawn at 0540; bilge 245; retarded clocks ½ hour for ZD+10; sunset at 1830; avg 6 kt; 143 mi, total sailed 3220 mi.
>
> **Feb 16**: tacking drill for starboard watch at 0032; 12 min. 40 sec to take in staysails, flying jib and main sail; bilge 325; Mate reports fleas in his cabin; rigging adjustments; avg 5.9 kt; 148 mi.
>
> **Feb 17**: sunrise 0535; bilge 300; at 1805 sighted Manihi Atoll 10 mi distant; sunset 1825; lookouts aloft; avg 5.4 kt; 130 mi; distance to Rangiroa Atoll 168 mi.
>
> **Feb 18**: on course for Rangiroa Atoll for emergency repairs; heavy rain squall; bilge 380, very oily; at 1820 Rangiroa Atoll in sight; lookouts aloft; avg 4.8 kt; 118 mi; dist. to Rangiroa, Tiputa 41 mi.

The increasing amount of water that needed to be pumped from the bilge was a clear indication of seepage. The oily condition of the bilge-water was worrisome in a different way – was the diesel leaking? If the *Monte Cristo* had scraped a coral reef, which abounded in those seas, it could have been disastrous. Everyone was on edge.

The heavy storms that built up all around them added to their worries. Jeff and Larry spoke about it in the skipper's cabin, leaning on the long table filled with charts.

"Skipper, I know we're pumping more water but…"

"Let me show you the log, Larry." Jeff had pushed the logbook toward him, slowing turning pages as he talked. "Whenever we ride a gale, the number of pumps it takes to clear the bilge increases a lot. Here – see my calculations."

Jeff shoved a sheet of paper toward him that had columns of numbers. "You can make a graph of it. With every gale, more bilge-water. And it doesn't go back down to an original low level in a calm. It ratchets up to a new high point. We have planks, probably starting at the garboard streak and higher, that are coming apart. This is not an optimal situation on the high seas, Larry."

Where talk on board had been about the marvelous adventures they were going to have once they reached Tahiti, now some were worried about making it there at all.

Rangiroa is in the Tuamotu, or *Dangerous*, Archipelago. The low atoll hides vast areas of coral that is sometimes closer to the surface because of tidal flow, than is safe for deep keeled ships like the *Monte Cristo*.

Safely passing through the reef meant they were wise to lay hove-to until the tide started ebbing from Rangiroa's huge lagoon.

In the traditional way, two of the new seamen were ordered to either side of the bow to swing lead lines to measure the channel depth. One man was right-handed, the other a southpaw. Sails were clewed up and the ship motored to carefully breast the current of Passe Tiputa to enter the vast, enclosed, inland salt-water lake. Once on the quiet lagoon, sails were set once again.

> Standing tall, as high as he could get on the mainmast, the visage of Captain Cook beamed, his chest swelling with fond memories of these crystal clear waters.

The ship sailed as if on a mirror, since the trade wind still caught her sails but nary a ripple marked the surface of the protected lagoon. It was magical.

They anchored off the meagre collection of shacks that comprised Tiputa Village. Jeff and Mike went ashore to clear customs.

For the first time since Ron had waved farewell from a beach in Mexico, Jeff was able to speak with Monte Cristo's owner by telephone. Ron Craig was relieved to learn that they were still in one piece. Jeff advised Ron that they were to sail soon to Papeete, Tahiti.

Figure 63 The goal: Tahiti, Feb. 1970

Liberty was granted to all but an unfortunate few of the crew. Entertainment facilities on the island consisted of an entrepreneur's ice chest set onto the beach, on which he served beer.

The rigors of the passage were soon forgotten when the guitars and bongo drums began, filling the air with their hypnotic rhythm. Music flowed and so did the beer. It seemed that Polynesians, of whatever island group they hailed from, never missed a chance for a beach party.

Nobody could remember at what point in the party it was, but all remembered a proposal that they should honour young Sam Bukema, Cabin Boy, who had turned thirteen that day. This information was translated to Mama-San who tended the bar. She disappeared for a few minutes and returned with her daughter in tow, also aged thirteen. She hoped that Sam would take advantage of this opportunity to learn the ways of love from a true island girl.

Lolita was all for it, but as soon as Sam realized what was planned for him he jumped up with a sudden gurgled "AH!", and made a beeline for the shore boat. In no time he was back aboard the *Monte Cristo*, with his innocence intact. Perhaps Sam would look back on that incident, as the years passed, with some regret.

On February 21st, ready to depart, *Monte Cristo* honoured Tiputa Village with a cannon salute.

In one of those coincidences that proved how small a world it is that we lived on, the only other yacht in Rangiroa was the Canadian sloop *Kalewa* of Vancouver, BC. They decided to sail together for the rest of the way to Tahiti for safety, since the way through the low islands of the Tuamotus Archipelago was rife with unpredictable currents.

Figure 64 The little deck cannon

The eyes of the crew all turned wistfully, as they could, to stare at the retreating atoll. Even Sam.

Larry was standing behind the young man. "Going to miss it, Sam?"

Quietly, "Yessir." Then, he quickly wiped an eye and added with some bravado, "It was a restful place and I'm very glad to have had the opportunity to experience it, sir."

> **Feb 22**: *Kalewa* close to port – warned by radio to keep clear; sighted Makatea Island port abeam 8 mi. at 0515; bilge 209; lost steerage way; engine lit at 800 rpm; *Kalewa* took station off starboard; sunset 1830; avg 3.5 kt; 97 mi total with 32 mi motoring.

Feb 23: 0000 motoring at 800 rpm; on course for Papeete; 0040 secured engine; squall approaching 0235; 0330 engine lit at 800 rpm; 0430 light sighted 2 points port; 0450 secured engine; hove to until sunrise; 0545 secured lights; set course for Papeete SSW½W; *Kalewa* alongside for photography; set royals; 1015 pilot aboard; engine lit to negotiate Papeete Pass; 1100 moored to Coaster Wharf, Papeete; Immigration and Custom inspectors aboard at 1115; avg 4 kt.

In contrast to the dry recitation in the ship's log, Jeff later wrote about the same approach to Tahiti:

"At first, the fabled isle appeared as a cloud lingering above the open sea. As we sailed closer all day, the speck of island rose from the sea to meet us, with craggy valleys revealing themselves shaded in purple haze. I recall the dramatic difference in hues from the deep blue of the ocean, to the paler blues and turquoise hues of the water on the island side of the reef, and the vivid greens of Tahiti's lush vegetation. Then also, we could smell the intoxicating aroma of the islands. Flowers, coconut oil, vegetation, all announced themselves before we even had a real glimpse of the island. We sailed still closer, and were inspected by a speedboat full of waving, French-speaking *popaas…*"

The harbour's official pilot guided them to their mooring, next to 14 yachts in various stages of seaworthiness.

Then, all seagoing order broke loose. Ron Craig came aboard, full of smiles and a chest of ice and beer. French

Figure 65 from "la Depeche de Tahiti"

Polynesian Customs and Health officials appeared. Miscellaneous people, who were unknown to the crew, wandered aboard. Brown-skinned kids climbed over the rail and started diving back into the water. Flower *leis* and *couronnes* were exchanged, and the party started. More guitars and bongos were produced and the music and frivolity began. The skipper was not in control of the situation any more. Tahiti was.

Tahiti has been a challenging test for many a ship's crew and master. How could a skipper hope to compete with the island's verdant beauty, joyful women and the smothering Garden of Eden appeal. In comparison to the grueling day-after-day labour aboard a sailing ship, where would *you* rather be? The Sirens were calling.

Here was the kicker at this point: the present crew – except for captain, mate, bosun, cook and engineer – all had been convinced by Ron Craig to pay for the priviledge of sailing aboard the *Monte Cristo*.

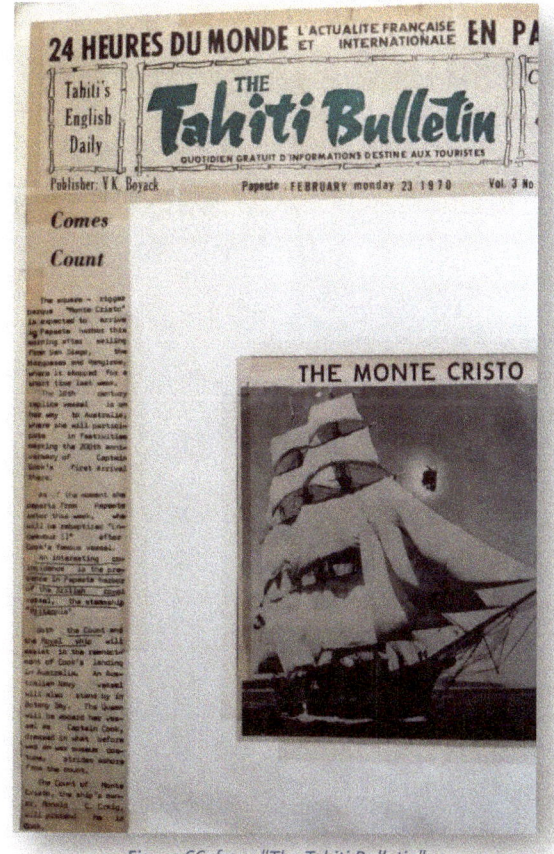

Figure 66 from "The Tahiti Bulletin"

No formal discipline could be applied, other than Jeff's periodic use of a mariner's acerbic tongue!

What To Do In Tahiti

There they were, moored next to the renowned *Quai Bir Hakkim*, where endless happy Tahitians, and just as many non-Tahitians who'd been captured by the Siren calls, all came to visit the *Monte Cristo*.

The first to leave the ship were those who heard the Siren song of Tahiti. Kathy Kelly, Bruce Doorly, and John Taylor went AWOL at 0900. Sam Bukema – who had originally intended to only go this far – and a disgruntled Ed Adams were released from the ship and cleared with the Port Captain and Immigration. As they were properly released, tickets were purchased for their return flight home to the US. Doorly and Taylor later, temporarily, returned to the ship.

The 28th of February proved to be a day of confrontation mixed with excitement. Jeff later wrote about that period:

> Film actor Marlon Brando came aboard to inspect the ship. He stayed for lunch and a few drinks and signed our guest book.
>
> "Jolly!" he inscribed.

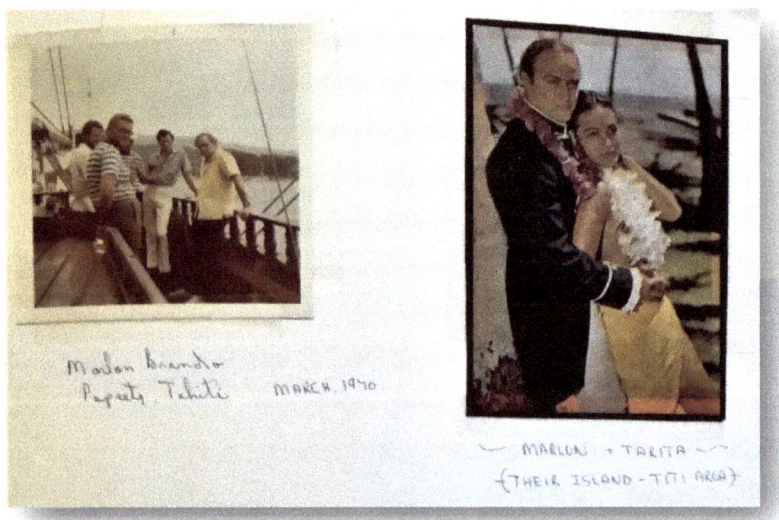

Figure 67 Brando allowed few pictures at that time

Brando first came to Tahiti in the early 1960s to make the MGM classic film *Mutiny on the Bounty*. He knew a bit about how to sail a square-rigger, which impressed me.

I asked Craig for more dollars so that we could do the urgent work on board. I was surprised when he refused. He didn't have enough cash and tried to evade the subject. This fact soon had spread to the rest of the crew, who, after mulling this disheartening news, on our fourth day in Tahiti, held an all hands bitch session ashore. They assembled beneath a shady casurina tree. I was not invited (or permitted) to attend this meeting. Each man and woman listed how much they had contributed to Ron Craig and the ship. They couldn't fathom how Craig could have run through all of this so quickly. Actually, he had spent $10,000 on provisions, half of which remained when we reached Tahiti. Also, airline tickets to the Society Islands were not cheap. Then, too, they had forgotten that we had pre-sailing expenses in California.

At this time, Marlon Brando became friends with Ron Craig. Brando wanted to have the *Monte Cristo* dock at his Island, Teti'aroa. They stayed in touch for awhile exchanging ideas but the heavy schedule of filming for *The Nightcomers* and then *The Godfather* drew away Brando's attention. They lost contact.

The diesel was then only working on five cylinders, having blown a fuel injector tip. It billowed embarrassingly large clouds of black smoke when it was used to charge the batteries.

More trouble on the horizon. Cyclone Emma was approaching and crews from all yachts and ships were desperately working to save their vessels. Some left for the high seas but it was agreed the *Monte Cristo* was not in shape to run. The crew of the *Monte Cristo* lashed their ship securely to the quay with three anchors deployed on the sea side. Old tires were lashed in bundles to cushion any surge that might push the ship into the stone and concrete quay. They were as ready as they could be.

Jeff made a point of noting to Ron, "Never in the short history of the barque *Monte Cristo*, had her crew worked so frantically, with such teamwork, for so long. I was proud of them."

From the log can be seen only the slightest glimpse of all that:

> **Feb 28**: In port; 0830 held all-hands session; several problems raised, personal and organizational; Marlon Brando aboard for a visit; Ron Craig departed for Canada and USA on business.
>
> **Mar 1**: no work on Sabbath.
>
> **Mar 2**: moored; Ed Adams and Sam Bukema departed for the USA on PanAm flight; cyclone reported 160 mi S; stowed for severe weather ay 1100.
>
> **Mar 3**: 0000 At Coaster Wharf, Papeete, Tahiti; at storm mooring awaiting possible 60 kt winds from Cyclone Emma; ship rigged down… Secured to Coaster Wharf by 14 mooring lines; Watch posted on deck; 0815 yacht *Alita II* preparing to get underway; Capt. And Papeete pilot informed by Mate Jefferies that bower anchor is across their hawse; *Alita II* got underway at 0845 assisted by 2 tugs; *Monte Cristo* lit off engine, slow ahead left rudder and slipped our cable to *Alita II*; cable taken aboard harbour tug and returned with anchor 0915; 1000 anchor ready to go again; awaiting docking of another vessel; wind light NE to N, intermittent squalls; engineer reports oil pressure issue and leak; 1100 Mate returned; weather moderating; 1130 wind and rain squall pushed ship against dock; hove in all lines and made fast to dock; 1300 Gaz de Tahiti delivered recharged propane tanks, $68 US; 1615 Bruce Doorly and Dr. Philip Groce announced they wish to leave the ship; intermittent showers, wind calming.
>
> **Mar 4**: 0000 Watch posted on deck following hurricane [cyclone] alert; weather at midnight light rain, wind calm; 1500 Bruce Doorly, Kathleen Kelly, Dr. Groce, Richard Hite released from ship; no word from Owner RC Craig; 1530 Capt. cleared crew visas at Immigration; sent telegram to Owner advising of situation.

Cyclone Emma hit them after sundown with sustained winds of 65 knots and much higher turbulent gusts. From the black sky, rain sheeted horizontally, relentlessly battering everything not bolted down. This lasted all night until 11 am the next morning. This was the last straw for some.

> **Mar 5**: 0800 pumped bilges 1300 strokes; Mate Michael Jefferies resigned; John Taylor, John Dye cleared from ship; signed aboard M/V Robert D. Conrad, research vessel; 1400 advised French authorities of ship's situation.
>
> **Mar 6**: 0900 above-noted crew saluted off; Ron Craig assigned $2500; sent wire to Banque de Tahiti; PanAm to have ticket waiting for Larry Williams; 1000, bank checked, no money.

That week was a royal mess on all fronts. Larry had finally gone to a doctor to see why his leg had not healed. It was found that his ankle had been broken in that incident when he had almost been electrocuted. Part of the money that Jeff was asking to be sent by Ron Craig was to pay for Larry's trip home so he could be looked after. Larry insisted on helping while waiting for the cash to arrive. That was his nature.

The other yachts moored nearby, if properly tied down, weathered it out. Some were in much worse shape. On land, Tahiti had been used to cyclones so they were well practiced in battening down.

For the *Monte Cristo*, the cyclone of March 4th pushed most of the crew to a hard decision.

Those who had worked so tirelessly to save the ship were shaken as they emerged on the 5th to look about. Despite having escaped structural damage, the crew were dismayed at what was done to everything above deck. Some of the sails, each of which had been taken down with their yards and carefully stowed on deck, had been picked up by the cyclonic winds and were left in tatters. Rigging was ripped and hung loose like vines from the masts.

All the work that had been put into adjusting the stays and rigging over the voyage since San Francisco had been torn asunder by the vicious storm.

It was going to take several weeks to refit the ship. But there was no money to do so and all their will was sapped. The last straw for many was that they appeared to be dead in the water without funds.

Figure 68 The Sirens Called

The *Monte Cristo* was in Tahiti for twenty-seven days. It was an emotional roller-coaster ride for all hands.

That seductive paradise, with Quinn's Bar next door on the dock and dancing girls in grass skirts flirting with the young men, was every bit as dangerous to seamen in the 1970s as were the Sirens calling to Sinbad's crew in ancient history.

In the end, with the devastating storm that ripped across their deck, it was that alluring presence of "Tahiti" that nearly scuttled the Australian adventure.

Paradise Aftermath

As friends departed and there were no funds to repair the damaged *Monte Cristo*, Jeff grew desperate. Ron Craig had left for Canada and the USA to raise money. He had continued to push the Australian officials about confirming their arrangement to use the *Monte Cristo* in their April celebrations.

Larry was waiting for his seat on a PanAm flight but he couldn't sit still. He spent every hour awake limping from one task to another on the tattered ship. On the morning of the *Monte Cristo's* thirteenth day in port, Larry awoke, hopped out of bed with his broken ankle, and stepped into eight inches of water sloshing around his cabin floor! Little else can get a sailor's heart racing faster!

Pumping, pumping – the water level was finally taken down to a manageable point. And then more pumping. The hand pump from a Lunenburg fishing boat work as it should. All hands participated in the pumping. A chalk board was set up to fairly record each person's contributions. It took 1300 strokes to clear the bilge that morning.

As soon as he found time, Jeff asked the advice of a nearby yacht captain, Ken Gau, of the American sailing fishing boat *Bluejacket*. Capt. Gau kindly offered to use his scuba gear to find the leak.

It turned out to be a broken main toilet discharge pipe. This had been encased in the poured concrete ballast so it could not have been found from inside. Sealed off by Capt. Gau, that leak stopped.

More good news came from Ron Craig. He had sent $2500 to a local bank to pay for supplies already received. Jeff gave $10 to each crewman, and he arranged for a party to raise their spirits. A few sailors from the USS *McMorris* (DW 1036) joined them, adding to the booze kitty. Contrary to local rumors, the *Monte Cristo* was not entirely in dire straits.

Next day, Larry Williams was sent off at the airport with two of the crew playing on guitar and singing Gordon Lightfoot's *Leaving on a Jet Plane*. Larry's departure set morale back down to a low depth.

With that, the remaining crew had another meeting on March 10th and came up with more demands. One of which was that the owner hire Drake Thomas again, who had been on the ship when it was on the California coast. The demands were transmitted by Jeff to Ron. On the telephone at the same time was another shareholder, Paul Haggard. They both promised to have the required new crew by Sunday.

In the meantime, more people signed on. Rigging was worked into shape. The local French Navy donated sails. Things started to look better for the weary crew. The Harbour Captain had been ordering the *Monte Cristo* to move every few days from one mooring position to another. While this was a major pain – having to down tools and rope for the repairs each time – it did keep the crew occupied with a variety of tasks.

Slowly, the *Monte Cristo* was reborn.

Rebirth

The next Sunday, March 15th, Ron arrived at the airport with Drake Thomas and Tom Money.

The uplifting news was that approval had finally been received from the Australians to pay for the *Monte Cristo* to be the feature ship in their Bicentennial Celebrations!

There were a few conditions. Chief among them was being able to sail to Botany Bay in time for the event.

Secondly, they had to change the ship's name to **Endeavour II**, in honour of Captain Cook's ship.

> With that news, the visage of the old captain, which had disappeared while the ship was in Tahiti, started to flicker back to life at the top of the mainmast. "By god! I had felt entirely swept away and all by that accursed cyclone! Come on lads! We have life again!"

A reinvigorated Jeff got to work calculating the possibilities. He drew up new rigging instructions and commissioned a local Tahitian woodcarver to chisel a set of nameplates for the bows and the stern.

There were naysayers left from the old crew who did not believe it possible to rerig the ship in time and to sail all the way to Sydney.

Jeff's calculations for the course had only one big question mark. They had to pass through the infamous area known as the *Doldrums*. A sailing ship needed wind, but the Doldrums, if they were caught in its grip, would give them none.

Being becalmed was termed *being in irons*, shackled like a prisoner.

What immediately came to mind was the Rime of the Ancient Mariner, by Samuel Taylor Coleridge, in which he recounts his misfortunes when becalmed:

> Day after day, day after day,
>
> We stuck nor breath nor motion;
>
> As idle as a painted ship,
>
> Upon a painted ocean…
>
> Water, water, everywhere,
>
> And all the boards did shrink;
>
> Water, water everywhere,
>
> Nor any drop to drink.

One of the first provisions Jeff ordered was plenty of water.

The recommended course to Australia, and the one planned out by Jeff, was to sail a total of 4550 miles. If they were ready to sail by March 21st, the thirteen mostly experienced sailors would make it. All they had to do was sail an average of 4.85 knots every day (!).

The good news as far as Jeff was concerned – echoed by Captain Cook's strengthening visage – was that the newly hired crew were all paid a wage. The remainder of the previous crew were those who had paid for their berths. Though this might produce rancour later, it was not a concern at that time.

Winds from Tahiti to Niue were brisk. They easily made an average of 6 knots most days, sometimes up to 7 knots. Entering the harbour at Niue on April 1st was tricky as the reefs could rip a large gash in the boards if the crew did not step smartly to orders.

Negotiating the entrance to the harbour, the white coral cliffs of the island were a welcome sight. They anchored before the settlement in Alofi Bay. Fifty-two hours of hectic work on further rigging repairs got the ship ready for the next stage, Niue Island to Suva, Fiji, which was 490 nautical miles.

The Postmaster asked Jeff if he would be kind enough to carry the mail to Suva. Agreeing to the simple request, Jeff was handed a Royal Mail flag. (Niue was still a British protectorate but was about to be made independent, like it not, as the British were at that time shedding their old Imperial possessions. Too costly, don't-you-know!)

It was during this time that the new name plate was mounted on the ship.

The *Honorary Royal Mail Ship Endeavour II* sailed from Niue on April 3rd.

On April 6th they found themselves in the Doldrums. Suva was still a long ways off. Jeff had plotted the course to intercept as little as possible of the Doldrums, but there they were.

Using several tricks discovered by mariners of yore, Jeff prepared the *Endeavour II* so that the instant a breeze should come up, sails were ready to grab some wind. To compound their troubles, the engine was out of commission. It was leaking oil. That meant their batteries were running down.

There was a portable generator. Using it foisted an unholy roar onto an already ill-at-ease crew and sent acrid plumes of smoke onto the deck. Jeff hit upon the idea of lashing the generator thirty feet up the mizzenmast. There, it was less objectionable as it charged up the batteries.

It was while becalmed at night that the Port Watch saw a sight that raised the hackles on the back of their necks.

In the Doldrums, not a wisp of air moved. The breakfast scraps thrown overboard in the morning could be seen off the stern the next day.

After the sun disappears in the Tropics the sea becomes an invisible **black**. New sailors who first see the deepness of the black step away from the edge of their ship, viscerally feeling like they were about to fall into a galactic black hole.

At 0400, becalmed and seemingly floating in deep space, a lookout said he thought he had made out a soft light. The skipper was called

Rebirth

from his bunk. The watch said he felt there was a greenish glow in the black pit of the water. Indeed, as Jeff and his new Mate, Drake Thomas, gazed into the distance, they could detect that the almost imperceptible current was taking them inevitably toward a glowing green-blue light in the sea.

There was nothing there – no ship, island or landing extraterrestrial (that they could see), except for the green-blue glow in the water. As the *Endeavour II* drifted toward the light, Jeff calculated that it was a column of about 300 feet in diameter and originated deep below.

Then, as the ship became encircled by the glow, everything transformed into a demonic, eerily glowing movie set. The people, the equipment, the masts and rigging, all glowed green-blue from the bottom up. It was terrifying.

Thankfully drifting further, the ship escaped from the glow.

If they hadn't been aware of the term "bioluminescence", the crew most certainly would have come up with a supernatural explanation. Even then, they felt their neck hairs stiffen for a long time before they stood down from frightened attention.

The next day, a breeze ruffled the ready canvas. It grew to a steady wind and they were off again.

Varying winds, squalls and possible reefs were met en route to Fiji's big island, Veti Levu. As they approached, a Fiji Airlines DC-3 buzzed them several times. It reported ahead so Jeff expected that there would be a welcoming party. However, when they tried to radio Suva Harbour, there was no answer.

Finally, a pilot came aboard to guide them into the anchorage. Their place at King's Wharf was not available, nor would it be until the next day. Flying the Royal Mail flag, Jeff thought they would have been given some privilege, but it took an adventure before they were able to hand over the mail bag and the flag to the Suva Postmaster.

Ron Craig met them on the pier. More good news. The Australians were anxious that the *Endeavour II* should be on time so a package of requested engine parts was waiting for them.

At the same time the engineer signed off with two more of the crew. A new engineer was quickly welcomed aboard, a Fijian named Walter Tripp.

Tripp was a marvel. Once underway he studied all the manuals then took apart every little piece of the old diesel. He cleaned and repaired and replaced everything that was needed. The engine purred to life at the first test.

Before leaving Suva, a large crowd had gathered on shore and started singing to the crew of the *Endeavour II*. It was not a standard raucous bellowing but, rather, the songs were delivered in beautiful three-part harmony. The crew, busy at the work of making ready to shove off, were staggered by the singing. Drake Thomas called to Jeff and said, "We have to sing something back."

Agreeing, Jeff ordered the nearby crew to begin a series of jobs that, in the old days, would have been accompanied by a sea shanty. Drake obliged by chanting out the classic, *"South Australia"*. The crew belted out the chorus:

> In South Australia I was born.
>
> *Heave away. Haul away.*
>
> South Australia, round Cape Horn.
>
> We're bound for South Australia…

The singing brought tears to a few eyes. A prominent section of the crowd was comprised of the gathering of relatives of Walter Tripp.

The pilot for the harbour passage was Capt. John Figgess. After they were safely past the near reefs, he and Jeff had a talk. A pilot boat had been maneuvering to come alongside to take Figgess and several passengers back to shore. Figgess took Jeff's hand.

"Captain Berry, I have become smitten by this vessel."

"Well, why don't you join us for the Sydney run?"

"By god…"

Figgess was on the VHS radio in a flash. He called his boss, who agreed to give him two weeks off. He called his wife who said something that appeared to be approval. At that, Figgess retrieved his gear from the pilot boat and joined the *Endeavour II*.

The final leg was to bring them to Sydney, after a gruelling 1730 nautical miles.

At April 12th, when they left Fiji, the crew consisted of:

Port Watch	Starboard Watch
Thomas, *Mate*	Berry, *Master*
DuMaurier	Smith
Springer	Caster
Collan	Figgess
Steers	Kohler, *Bosun*
Mitchell	Higgins
Money	Tripp, *Engineer*
Tero Raa, *Cook*	

Figure 69 from Fiji Times. Coincidences.

Apollo 13 re-entered on April 18 over the Pacific between New Zealand and Fiji

Unlike those on shore and around the world, who were being given fascinating details about NASA's newest voyage to the Moon, the crew of the *Endeavour II* had heard nothing about that other crew flying far above them.

That is, until April 17th. Well recorded in history was the story of NASA scientists and technicians, desperately working to keep their astronauts alive and bring them back safely to Earth. Once it was determined that there was a likelihood of such a safe return, the course they plotted was to have the Command Module re-enter the atmosphere somewhere over New Zealand or Fiji. At the same time, the Soviets were scrambling every "research" vessel they had to get to that area. The Russians offered to "help" the Americans by picking up the crew and Command Module from the sea (and incidentally go over and take pictures of every component).

Rebirth

All US-friendly ships in the area were contacted, asked that they watch out for Soviet vessels and intercept if necessary, so that the Apollo 13 crew and Command Module should not fall into Soviet hands.

That request was made of the *Endeavour II*. Therefore, on April 18th, the sailing ship *Endeavour II* posted watches for things streaking from the sky within their assigned quadrant of the Pacific.

Figure 70 The Russians Are Coming!
per Australian Associated Press-Reuter

As there was no procedure for retrieval of space ships by a wooden 3-masted barque, Jeff and Drake were just as happy not to have sighted such a phenomenon.

Back to regular sailing, the ship was in luck with steady winds that allowed them to fairly fly the miles toward Sydney. Average speeds were occasionally recorded in excess of 11 knots – almost unheard of. However, that constant hard work against the waves and blustery winds were opening up the ship's timber seams below the waterline, and rattling every loose yard and stay above the deck. The ship's design had never been meant to take that day-after-day pounding.

The differences between a solid Whitby coal-carrying ship that Captain Cook sailed and the comparatively delicate *Monte Cristo/Endeavour II* lay in the robustness of the wood used, the considerably greater number of braces, gussets and shorings within the hull of a working ship, and in the material used above deck. It was taking at least 700 strokes to clear the bilges. Were it not for the constant sweat and toil of the dedicated crew, the ship would soon become a pile of timber floating someplace on the southern ocean. Much as the crew of Apollo 13 sweated to force their reluctant collection of technological parts to swing them past the Moon and back down to Earth, the crew of the *Endeavour II* daily performed minor miracles to keep their vessel sailing bravely toward Oz.

The *Endeavour*'s skipper took the night watch. Jeff and Mate Drake decided that Drake and the six seamen of the Port Watch would be best employed in daytime sailing duties, while the Starboard Watch would maintain the course and also do the detailed navigation that was essential to steer the most efficient course. Each night Captain Figgess and Master Berry had astro–navigation competitions to see who came closest to their exact geographical position. Neither were ever off more than a few miles.

By April 21st, the wind picked up to a brisk eighteen to twenty-five knots from the NNW in a still-moderate sea. They were sailing at a very respectable eight point six knots when a pair of Royal Australian Air Force P2V Neptune patrol bombers swooped out of the sky and started circling the ship.

Rebirth

That was the *Endeavour II*'s first direct contact from the Australian mainland. The bombers buzzed at masthead height as the pilots chatted with Jeff and Drake on the wireless, then they ran directly at the ship, only to split and pass down each side at the last moment. The pilots were having a wonderful time!

Figure 71 Picture by the Royal Australian Air Force

The mariners hoisted their flag aft, and set all sail, then tried to appear blasé about being the centre of so much attention.

Later, the RAAF presented the ship with a series of spectacular photos of one bomber over *Endeavour II*, while they had been sailing at almost maximum speed. It was the best shot of *Endeavour II* ever taken. The next morning, that photo was splashed over the front pages of most of the daily newspapers in Australia. They were getting close. At noon they were an estimated fifty-eight miles from Sydney Heads.

The Queen Was (not) Pleased

On April 23rd, at 2400, Jeff wrote in the log:

> 2315: Secured anchor detail. Set anchor watch. Hoisted "Q" flag on stbd yardarm. Notified Owner R.C. Craig of *Endeavour II*'s arrival.
>
> 2400: Secured auxiliary. It has been a very long haul from San Diego – total 100 days – 64 days underway, 7429 miles, for a daily average of 116 miles per day, or 4.7 knots.
>
> I should like to note the competence, hard work and professionalism displayed by the crew of *"Monte Cristo/Endeavour II"* during this Passage. Well Done!
>
>   J. F. Berry, Master

A Q flag indicates "quarantine", until cleared by a designated doctor. This is routine for ships first entering a port from afar.

Having made a spectacular passage from Fiji to Sydney under conditions that would have been daunting to mariners of any age, the crew of the *Endeavour II* might have expected the occasional applause from a crowd on shore.

What they were told, instead, was to hide. They were too early.

The ship was directed by Ron Craig to follow the strict instructions of the Australian Navy. Now that they were within sight of their goal, little things started to go wrong. A log line was fouled on the rudder while they were tacking off Sydney Head. The fore topsail sheet was carried away. And they were commandeered by the Australian Navy.

Told to moor amongst some oil tankers, they were subsequently shuffled to a remote dock. Meanwhile, the crew's great expectations of a grand welcome in Sydney had to be suppressed. It was not easy after the ceaseless work and sacrifice to make it to the party on time, then to be told to take the servants entrance after a delay and please be quiet about it.

The next day may have been a Sunday – the 26th of April – but there would be no rest. The ship had to be made to look its best in its new role as the symbol of Colonial Discovery. All those modern things that had helped them survive the ocean voyage need to be removed or hidden away: fuel drums, life rafts, a motorcycle (for shore leave), spare stores, storage bins and non-18th century clothing. The ship needed to be ready to receive visitors.

The ship was then shuttled once again, being ordered to sail into Botany Bay to a temporary berth at the end of a long seawall away from public eyes. In the process of being secured to their berth and before they could ask for a directions to the nearest pub, an Australian Navy staff car drew up as close to the ship as it could get. Out stepped a figure in a brilliant white uniform. This youthful Navy Lieutenant was an Admiral's Aide-de-Camp.

The officer walked down the seawall, shooting a few photos as he came. He carried an attaché case. When he reached *Endeavour II*, he requested permission to come aboard. Jeff greeted him.

"I am Aide-de-Camp to Admiral Victor Smith. The Admiral is in charge of the naval review and re-enactment ceremony at Botany Bay, before H.M. tomorrow." (H.M. meant *Her Majesty*, of course.)

"The Admiral has decided that this is too important a ceremony to risk letting civilians cock it up. Therefore, we are herewith commandeering the Canadian Barque *Endeavour II* and her crew for a period not to exceed fourteen days.

"This vessel will be under the operational control of the R.A.N. during this time."

A look in Jeff's eyes might have prompted the next comment. "No, we're not paying you. We will award you, the Master, a temporary commission as a Sub-Lieutenant, non-pay status. I strongly suggest that you and your crew obey our orders closely and fully, Captain."

He then made it clear the crew would be under naval discipline during this time, subject to courts-martial if anyone got out of line in the slightest.

With a slight smile, Jeff asked, "What should we call the ship?"

"*HMAS Endeavour II*. She is being commissioned into the R.A.N. as a naval auxiliary."

When the orders were presented to the crew, the Aide-de-Camp was surprised to learn that only one of the crew was actually Canadian. After a thoughtful pause he carried on with the commandeering.

Jeff, on later reflection, believed that the whole exercise had all been bluff on the part of the Australian admiral. He didn't think the Admiral had explicit permission to commandeer the ship, but he nonetheless did so, and got away with it.

And that was how a Yank ended up an officer in the Royal Australian Navy, if only unofficially, for fourteen days. Jeff's mother had always wanted her son to be a military officer like his dad. He had finally made it, in a circuitous fashion.

In the spirit of the occasion, Jeff purchased a British Merchant Service Master's uniform jacket and hat. The main thing he remembered about it was that it was damned expensive.

The official Bicentenary ceremony was to have been a sober re-enactment of the arrival and landing, 200 years ago, of Captain Cook, played by Australian actors. It was a shame that two university students, one dressed more or less as Captain Cook, slipped to shore before Her Majesty and the assembled dignitaries, to perform their own version of the landing.

The crew of the *Endeavour II* had front row seats and enjoyed the whole event enormously. At first, they quietly observed, then they joined in with the onshore crowd's raucous cheering as the police and military pursued the university students back and forth across the sandy shore.

After the entertainment of chasing down and hauling off the interlopers, the cocked-up official ceremony was restarted.

H.M. had deliberately, studiously, ignored the antics of the students.

Endeavour II's post-ceremony welcome ashore was a heady round of picture opportunities, speeches and the glitz and glamour usually afforded to entertainment celebrities.

The first few hours of explaining for the hundredth time to each of the adults and children in the lineup of visitors went like this: "This ship is only similar in size and in the use of three masts to Captain Cook's ship, and, no, the good Captain was not a jailer so there were no criminals from England chained up tween-decks."

Soon, the crew's appreciation of celebrity changed.

Figure 72 from the Sydney Sun

How Celebrity Works

Figure 73, the ship's sponsor, The Sydney Morning Herald

Ron Craig had an agreement with the newspaper, *Sydney Morning Herald*. They, in turn, appeared to take direction from the political party in power. So long as the public had their eye on the ship, the *Endeavour II* would receive support. It was inevitable that, unless media appearances were regularly managed and the public was given a continual feeding of exciting news about the ship and her crew, attention would fade. When that fade inevitably set in, support would dissolve away.

Life aboard proceeded more prosaically than one might expect. Prior to the Bicentenary, Ron and Jeff had to practice such archaic tasks as the proper forms of Court etiquette for British Royalty, prime ministers, less-than-prime ministers, visiting presidents, and city mayors, as well as religious leaders of several faiths. After the event, Jeff was able to focus on the pressing matters of repairing their ship after the pounding she received in her headlong run from Tahiti.

Figure 74 Ron Craig and bewigged Jeff Berry, Mate Thomas with Tero Raa

It took Ron a short time to acclimatize to the Australian business and entertainment situation.

Once the immediate celebrity of the Bicentenary began to wane, Ron arranged for the ship to be featured in the city proper. They sailed from Botany Bay to Sydney, berthing at historic Circular Quay.

Here were ancient dockside warehouses that used to host innumerable wool clippers that sailed their goods to England a hundred years previously. It was a stone's throw from the brand new Sydney Opera House. The place was buzzing with happy visitors.

The routine would have the morning crew wash down, preparing for the crowds; two daytime sessions of tours and answering questions; then, the evening crew would clean up until midnight; Ron and his hard working wife Dorothy would take another two hours counting what became heavy bags of coins for a bank deposit to be made the next day. There were speeches to be made at business luncheons, television hosts to speak to and dinners to attend. Ron was the indefatigable organizer while the ship's officers and some of the seamen were put up front to the public. Locals were hired to control the crowds.

At May 5th, the skeleton crew of the *Endeavour II* were:

Jeff Berry, *Master*	Drake Thomas, *Mate*
Walter Tripp, *Engineer*	Tero Raa, *Cook*
Douglas DuMaurier	John Springer
Maureen Higgins	

Seamen were added to crew over the next few days while they were moored in Sydney. Watches were careful at that time to detect university student pranks, as they had been emboldened by the antics of the two students who had botched the Bicentenary Celebrations.

A log notation on May 11th stated that the new cook, Maureen Higgins, was employed for a monthly salary of $240.

The Beach Boys were welcomed aboard on May 12th. Their publicity manager had arranged for filming and pictures on the ship.

Perhaps just as notably, on the 14th, the ship's new *head*, all bright brass and impressive, was put into operation.

Passing by in a comfortable Royal Australian Navy launch on May 18th, Canadian Prime Minister Pierre Elliot Trudeau and Australian PM John Gorton waved at the Master and seamen of the *Endeavour II*. PM Trudeau shouted a greeting as the ship's colours were dipped. Meanwhile, repairs were being made and new equipment was installed.

The Canadian PM showed his willful personality at this time. He was invited aboard the ship. For some reason he refused to do so unless *Monte Cristo* were closer to where he was to access it. That maneuver would have been much more complicated than the PM could have known. This was not a canoe or a motor launch. Moving the square-rigger would have taken considerable time and trouble so Ron Craig stated that he wouldn't do this, particularly since neither the PM nor the Canadian government would acknowledge the unique accomplishments of the *Monte Cristo*. No help or recognition had been offered during their outstanding journey to the Bicentenary Celebrations, even while the ship was promoting Canada. Such recognition still has not been given. Did Trudeau feel affronted? One wonders how long that petty attitude by government officials will last.

By May 21st, the crew of the *Endeavour II* consisted of:

- Jeff Berry, *Master*
- Drake Thomas, *Mate*
- Walter Tripp, *Engineer*
- Maureen Higgins, *Cook*
- Douglas DuMaurier
- John Springer
- Ashton Fox
- Peter Duff
- Robert Carey (the lone Canadian)

Two days later, several more crewmembers were added:

- Dr. Byron Rigby
- Anna Rigby
- Jeff Rigby
- Christopher Scott

How Celebrity Works

Arrangements were made for the following to join the crew within a month:

    David Salt   Desmond Kearns, *Bosun*

    Susan Kearns

While in Sydney, a number of crewmembers joined as others left.

Several incidents happened about which Jeff was not disposed to write home to his mother.

There was that time when the mob came calling to demand protection money. The mobsters were convinced, after a heated exchange from Jeff and Drake, to "bugger off".

A coterie of camp followers, male and female, began to hang out with some of the sailors, who took pains to retell perhaps exaggerated stories to the other crew members of their adventures with delightful individuals from the coterie. That group followed the ship in their cars along the coast, going from port to port.

And there was the case of one sailor who was convinced to spend an exciting time with two beautiful young ladies of the night, who happened to be identical twins…

More seriously, the question of what could be done with their valuable fame was only raised once by Jeff. Ron admitted that business contacts wanted the ship to continue on to the UK, replicating Captain Cook's return voyage, and they were pressuring him to decide. He asked Jeff if he would be confident enough to sail around the Cape of Good Hope to England.

Several moments of serious thought were needed by Jeff before he replied that it could be possible, if a series of significant repairs were made. However, Jeff recommended, instead, that the major asset that Ron's ship currently had was her fleeting fame. Once that faded, her value decreased day-by-day. If Ron and his other business interests wanted to carry on with the adventures of a sailing vessel like Cook's, they could use the funds from a sale of *Endeavour II* to build a real duplicate Whitby collier.

Figure 75 In Sydney, from government tourist info

However, Ron grew upset. "Sell this beautiful ship? Absolutely not! It is only this ship and what she has done that carries any value!"

"Sir, the *Monte Cristo/Endeavour II* may well be written of in grand terms in the newspapers, but it was only with the daily sweat and toil of her crew that enabled her to sail through dangerous seas, even as far as Tahiti, much less on our grueling run to Sydney."

Ron was not convinced. "Tell me, honestly, Jeff; how long can this ship continue sailing?"

Another considered pause by Jeff. "I would say less than ten years."

"What! The materials are the best Canadian timber…"

> Unseen since the Celebrations, the visage of Captain Cook shimmered into view in a corner of Jeff's cabin where Ron and Jeff were speaking. He had nodded sadly at the list of this ship's deficiencies. On hearing Jeff mention building a real Whitby collier, the glow from the old Captain would have lit the room, had there been children to see it.

Politely shaking his head, Jeff used his fingers to list off points. "The *Monte Cristo*, as designed and built by Brigola, did not follow standard marine engineering practices; the materials used for her main structure needed to be hardwood not softwood; the design flaws we have discussed – mast location, resulting rigging issues, keel shape and run, ballast, engine, rudder, mechanical systems and her lack of designed purpose which caused so many compromises below deck…"

Ron had heard it all before and grew exasperated at being reminded. "Yes yes. Fine. She has a few issues. But I've paid a lot of money to correct most of those. You are too negative about this ship, Jeff. I don't know…" Reality was beginning to percolate through.

Ron thought for a moment. "Ok. Find us a shipyard here in Sydney that can do the repairs. Let me contact my people."

It was decided that after the Sydney work was done, the ship would be sailed north to Newcastle do further refitting. After that, more money would be raised by visiting what Ron called the main population centres up the east coast, before crossing to New Zealand. After New Zealand, Ron would reconsider a possible sale.

Captain and crew had their orders. The rest of their time in Sydney was a hectic rush of dealing with the crowds and doing endless repairs during any slack time.

In a distracted state, with his mind overfull of practical things, Jeff was presented with a remarkable relic. In Jeff's words:

> Aboard stepped a middle-aged man who brought with him what I consider was a real magical moment. I have regrettably

forgotten his name and nationality, although I think he was either British or Australian. My visitor brought with him a worn, sea-stained, wooden box with dove-tailed edges and brass corner protectors. It was of the type that used to hold nautical navigation instruments aboard ships----sextants, octants, quadrants, bearing circles, sun compasses, and other similar devices that were in use about two hundred years ago. The man asked to see me, then opened the box to reveal an exquisitely crafted brass instrument of a type I had not seen before (or since, for that matter). It looked a bit like a bearing circle that might fit around a magnetic compass, in that it was divided into degrees of arc along the horizontal ring. It had another brass circle, also subdivided into degrees, that was mounted inside the first ring that was hinged to pivot vertically to a 90 degree angle. This allowed the navigator, I assumed, to crudely sight the angle of the heavenly body he was interested in. Just as he would with an astrolabe or a quadrant. I remember that, engraved into the brass of this instrument, there were adjustment marks for the month and day, meaning the declination of the Sun. It was not exactly an astrolabe, which I've never seen actually used, and it had no mirrors, so it was not an octant or sextant. Since it could be used around a magnetic compass, I think it was a sort of well-crafted navigator's quadrant combined with a bearing circle. It could slip over a compass and act as a bearing circle. I remember thinking that it looked extremely intricate in the same manner that ancient brass watches are complicated, with escapements and gears, all doing different things. Any person who mastered this instrument would be a master navigator indeed, I thought. This navigation instrument was something far outside my league. Its owner showed me a handwritten booklet, yellowed with age. The booklet was in the bottom of the box and was a seemingly complete instruction manual for this instrument. It was penned in flourishing Spenserian 18th Century script. The ink on the yellowed pages was faded by age. On the last page was a note by the author, which stunned me. I have forgotten the exact wording, but paraphrase it from memory like this:

> *The Author was Late Master of H.M Armed Transport Bounty, on a voyage from Portsmouth to the South Seas to collect a Cargo of Breadfruits and thence to transport these fruits to divers Plantations in the West Indies isles. As fortune had it, this voyage was Abruptly interrupted by the Illegal and Piratical Seizure by Disloyal Members of the ship's crew. We, the Loyal Members, numbering 19 men in all, were banished to the Ship's Pinnace, with provisions and water for but five days. We were allowed only a compass and this instrument, with some nautical tables to find our way. We sailed slightly less than 4,000 miles in 48 days, through treacherous seas and cannibal isles before reaching safety in the Dutch Port of Batavia on Java Isle, with only one man being lost, and he to savages on Tiputa Isle.*
>
> Signed: *Wm. Bligh, Lt. Royal Navy, and late Master of HM Armed Transport Bounty*
>
> Dated: March, 1790 Portsmouth

The owner told me he had found this instrument in a junk shop in England and had purchased it for a ridiculously small amount just before World War II. I offered him five times that amount, but he just laughed as he carefully replaced it in its well worn box.

When reading Capt. William 'Breadfruit' Bligh's booklet, I felt a chill that reached across the centuries from Bligh to me. This almost sacred relic spoke to me.

Jeff was not quick enough to obtain the relic.

Has it resurfaced?

Ashore, Ron was fully absorbed in dealing with one financial problem after another, while Jeff had to find creative ways to cut on-going costs aboard.

On June 8th, Ron and Dorothy needed to fly to Vancouver, Canada, on business and to raise funds for the ship.

They returned to Sydney on July 12th.

Meanwhile, income from visitors did not keep pace with the cost of needed repairs. Ron had arranged for a progress payment plan with Woodley's Slipway shipyard in Sydney based on "half the take from visitors". Combined with the salaries, food and moorage fees, the business side of the ship was not doing well. Each week that their fame faded, the visitors line got shorter. Jeff was concerned that the option of a successful sale of the ship was slipping away. Nevertheless, he didn't bring that topic up again.

On the Tasman Sea

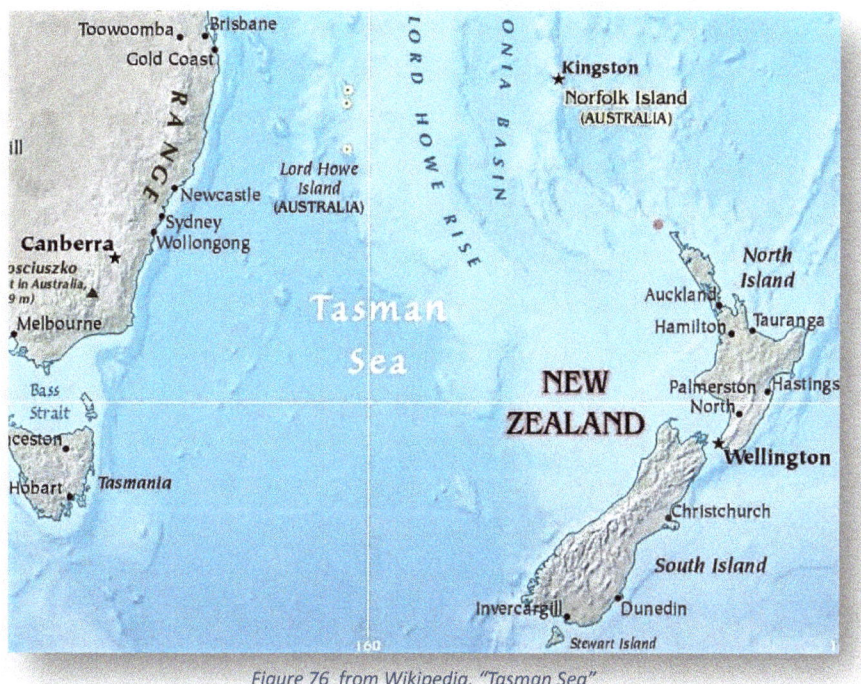

Figure 76 from Wikipedia, "Tasman Sea"

Work done in Sydney harbour allowed the *Endeavour II* to sail, in a fashion, north to Newcastle for further work.

As the *Endeavour II* approached the end of the dark blue ocean waters off Newcastle, the ship had one solemn task to perform. They carried the ashes of an old Australian seaman, a "Cape Horner", who had passed on a week before.

Previously, the veteran of sailing 'round Cape Horn had insisted on a visit to the grand ship in Sydney as his final outing in life. Fully satisfied, he died shortly after. His children had his remains cremated. They asked Skipper Jeff that the *old Salt's* ashes be buried at sea.

The ship was stopped just outside of soundings, where the water was deep and intensely blue, as was standard practice for sea burials. Jeff mustered all hands in their full *Captain Cook* regalia, to honour the late Able Seaman Francis Alexander Luks. The Queen Anne ensign was lowered to half staff. Above it was a shimmering, solemn Captain Cook, head bowed. The skipper read the moving *Burial At Sea* section from the ship's Church of England Book of Common Prayer. Grey gritty ashes were scattered by Ron in the breeze to leeward. Some particles floated for awhile above the sea surface. A random gust blew them back to dust part of the poop deck.

In carrying out this final act, they had followed the family's wishes and buried Francis Luks' remains in the bosom of the deep with proper respect and solemnity.

After the burial, the *Endeavour II* proceeded into Newcastle for the next round of repairs and refitting.

Figure 77 Postal proof

Costs were mounting. Payments were being made for the Sydney shipyard work, and the Newcastle bill was expected to be heavy.

It was at that vulnerable time that two of the crew decided to foment discontent. Secretly trying to influence the older crew, without having the courage to first speak with Ron or Jeff, they said that they deserved a larger cut of the mounds of cash coming in. The two said they should have more control over the ship's operations. And one of them wanted Jeff's job.

Speaking with Ron one evening at his hotel in Newcastle, Jeff advised the ship's owner of the rumblings he had heard about.

"Sir, this is a difficult conversation for me. A crewman, who wishes to remain anonymous, has told me that there are two people who have been secretly speaking to the others. While I personally feel that is a cowardly approach, I believe you need to hear what they have been saying."

Ron listened then nodded. "I suspected as much. I expect it's the same two who've asked to see me tomorrow night."

Jeff was visibly unhappy with this topic. "Right. Some of the crew are, I regret to say, upset with the meager amount of stipend they are receiving. It seems not to be the opinion of everyone. As you well know, for my part, I did not sign on as skipper to become rich. My commitment has been, always, to do the right thing by this ship. She requires special care so, I suppose, I feel a compassion toward this limping lady. If either of those two really want my job I am prepared to pack my seabag and go walkabout, as they say here."

Ron shook his head. "No no. This will not do, Jeff. I do not need somebody telling me how to run my business. We've been through too much in this enterprise to give it up to some rabble rouser with too great an opinion of himself."

The next evening Ron told the two the same thing. They then stomped away, vowing to make things bad for the ship and her owner.

On September 1st, *Mate* Drake Thomas and Maureen Higgins went off in their vile mood, apparently on a private trip to the Outback. They left a crew mumbling with discontent.

Despite the backroom politics, the *Endeavour II* still needed critical repairs to be completed. Ron struggled to raise money for the work, suffering legal demands from the shipyard to hold his vessel in port until bills were paid.

Only some of the crew had bought into the demands for more pay and control. The mix on board had changed considerably after they arrived in Oz. Fewer than half of those who had been aboard from Tahiti were still with the ship, with the others being recent Australian and British seamen who had been drawn to the real-life adventure of sailing a square-rigger. Some of the new crew were experienced canvas sailors but they all had a different attitude from the American crew. The new folks were quite ready to work hard to accomplish the many technical and tedious tasks that needed doing on an historical vessel. Professional pride trumped financial questions.

Finally, it was not divulged how, but Ron was able with deft financial manipulations to satisfy the Newcastle shipyard.

After a long forced stay in the old harbour, the *Endeavour II* was free to carry on, sailing to Coffs Harbour on September 1st. Coffs was half way up the coast toward Brisbane.

That was to be a trip that taxed the abilities of crew and ship to the extreme.

The Tasman Sea has a reputation among mariners. When winds come from the Antarctic they are called a "Southerly Buster". Once away from Newcastle, the gales that slammed into the *Endeavour II* very well fit the description of **Buster**.

The ship endured sheets of driving rain and thirty-five knot winds for an intolerable eight hours. Waves turned into valleys of roiling water. The bilges needed constant pumping by exhausted crew.

On September 3rd, gusts reached sixty-five knots and the swells were measured at twenty feet from trough to crest. The crew were badly drained from non-stop labour just to stay afloat. Their expressions all

On the Tasman Sea

showed the fear that any grown person should exhibit in those conditions.

> Even the ghost of Captain Cook clung in desperation to a mast as the horizonal gale whipped his coat.

As Jeff would later write:

> I remember bracing myself on the poop and looking at the sweep of the deck as the hull would first be kicked in the stern by a wave, which would then sweep under us. When this happened, the bow and bowsprit lie about parallel to the surface of the wild sea. Then *Endeavour II* would make her torturous climb, pointing to the clouds. We were hobby horsing fore and aft, but we held on. Barely. I wondered about the strength of the hull yet again. I remember the builder in Canada, Alex Brigola, boasted that his ship's hull was exceptionally strong as built, since the hull was triple-planked with mahogany, with sealing between each ply. I questioned that.

Indeed, later, it would be revealed that the construction was well below par, with simple nails holding the planking together. It was a miracle that kept her together on the Tasman.

By September 5th, the *Buster* had died down and the battered ship and her thoroughly beaten up crew were able to sail in clear waters to Coffs Harbour.

Moored and safe, the next day was spent cleaning up after the effects of riding up and down the heart-stopping white-water roller-coasters. During the storm, the crew had grabbed what few rations they could, as they briefly went below. Safely in harbour, the mess that greeted them was not pleasant. Most of their provisions tween-decks had been crashing about, along with everything else not screwed down. Veggies were found hidden everywhere.

One of the crew saw the bright side, "The good news is that the bilge water didn't contaminate the food. We were leaking so heavily in the storm that all the bilges were clean washed out with salt water!"

Someone else suggested that they could leave the hidden potatoes until they sprouted – they would be found easier with their stems growing toward the light.

Coffs Harbour had a claim to fame. It boasted the world's largest banana. With the famous *Endeavour II* in town, locals, therefore, had the option of entertaining themselves by viewing the huge yellow concrete banana or paying for a tour of the *Endeavour II*. A few did pay to see the vessel that had recently saluted the Queen.

It didn't take long for Ron to realize that the "population centres" along Australia's northeast coast might be slim pickings for his business plan. He decided to carry on to Brisbane, then consider later if they were to sail to New Zealand.

Once more under sail over a then calmer Tasman Sea, the *Endeavour II* pushed north toward the hot Brisbane coast.

Their Brisbane approach was particularly difficult. They had to make their way up Moreton Bay and the meandering Brisbane River. As a

Figure 78 Bustard Head Lighthouse - per News Corp Australia

On the Tasman Sea

training exercise, Jeff had the crew sail rather than motor most of the way. That decision may have been prompted by the fact that the local pilot on board, Captain Sharp, had sailed with one of Jeff's heroes, Captain Villiers, on the renowned sailing vessel *Conrad*. The crew went through endless evolutions and got quite good at tacking in narrow confines.

The Brisbane crew picture belies the tensions seething below:

Figure 79 Brisbane crew

Top row, left to right: David Salt, Chris Scott, Keith the Shipwright, Annette his wife, Stu, Crash the engineer, Robert Carey a Canadian, Dr. Byron Rigby.

Lower row, left to right: Doug du Maurier, Peter Duff, John Springer, Janet the Doctor's wife.

Plastered in Brisbane

The city of Brisbane was their last chance to make enough money to pay off all the debts. If they could get out from under that yoke, Ron figured the *Endeavour II* would be free to sail to New Zealand, then, perhaps, he would sell the ship.

Ron tried everything he could on the dock to promote the ship. He hired a red-coated 18th-Century town crier with tricorne hat to ring his bell and publicly announce the arrival from the southern colony of New South Wales, of the "Most excellent newly-built barque *Endeavour II*". That plan brought in a trickle of weekend visitors.

They tried to put on a bit of a show on weekends. As weather and winds permitted, they would set sail while moored at the dock to attract passers-by. The impressive show of canvas did bring some paying customers.

Ron also contacted several outlying school districts that started bussing in students to visit for historical tours. During these tours the crew clad in buckled shoes, silk stockings, periwigs and all.

The weeks ground on as repairs were done by local firms.

Ron and Jeff, along with several new Aussie backers, came up with a grand plan to sell subscriptions to support the ship. The subscribers were to be called *honorary crew members*. A few dollars bought a visitor a vicarious berth aboard, as an honourary Seaman. A few dollars more and the lucky person could be an honourary Mate. A little more and he could have the skipper's job, honourary Captain.

The plan was to write a monthly issue of the *"Endeavour II's Log"*, which was to be an eight-page publication that would document in melodramatic prose their adventures as they sailed the seas. Jeff wrote the first *Master's Column*. That plan was not an overwhelming success since they lacked funds to advertise and distribute it properly.

Ron had several meetings with the crew in which he put his cards on the table telling them the amounts owed to each person or company. He laid out their immediate prospects for clearing the debts and what he, as the Owner, was doing to keep his dream afloat. Jeff and others who had known Ron longer were impressed. Faced with mounting financial woes, Ron demonstrated a growth in leadership that had not been fully appreciated before. His message was that they needed to hang tough and hang together as a crew.

Then came the revenge of the *wanna-be*s. On the afternoon of October 20th, 1970, after twenty-four days in port, Queensland law officers visited to plaster writs on the main mast.

"In the name of Her Majesty, Queen Elizabeth II, the Queen of Australia, you are hereby arrested and detained until the following debts are discharged…", the archaic legal language read. This was courtesy of former crewmen Drake Thomas, Maureen Higgins, Desmond Kearns, John Chappel (who had only resigned that morning) and Stuart Smith. The ship was legally chained to the dock until they came up with $6,010 Australian dollars.

Ron was angry beyond words when he heard of the ship's arrest.

Jeff went through a feeling of deep despair. Had they gone through so much travail, dangerous sailing and disappointment for it all to end like this?

Ron was incensed that the Engineer and seaman, in particular, would participate in such a thing, after all the trouble the crew had surmounted to get this far, and after all the work they were still doing to clear their debts. Angrily, he kicked them off the ship. They

Plastered in Brisbane

scurried away quietly, certainly embarrassed. Perhaps they were ashamed by what they had wrought.

Significantly, there was no mass exodus of crew. David Salt lightened the mood when he stencilled broad arrows across his white shirt and fashioned a leg iron with fake ball and chain. A true P.O.M.E. (Prisoner Of Mother England), Dave dragged it all over the main deck, to the amusement of the remaining crew. This action raised their spirits.

The next day, they received the second blow: the Supreme Court of Queensland announced the arrest of the ship for the outstanding sum

Figure 80 Endeavour II in Australia

Plastered in Brisbane

of approximately A$9,000, demanded by the Woodley Slipway in Sydney and a machine shop, Storey and Keers. This amount would climb over the next few days to more than A$48,000 in total, as word spread and creditors climbed on board. Included were mortgage payments in Canada that were overdue.

And, they were not earning enough to keep them in daily rations. It was to the credit of the crew that morale, despite all that, remained high.

On October 21st, the ship's log notes that they "opened negotiations with D Thomas' solicitors in Sydney via telephone".

At a meeting with the crew later, those who wished to take work ashore were encouraged to do so. The crew themselves agreed to take a painting job, then give the *Endeavour II* 65% of their salary while in Brisbane.

So many things did not go well for the ship in Brisbane. While unrelated to the other events aboard, the day after she came aboard on November 8th, a new recruit named Jane Handy was found in her cabin in a pool of blood. She had attempted suicide as a result of a crisis in her personal life. She was discovered in time to be bandaged by the crew and placed in an ambulance. Jane did survive that incident.

Ron kept trying to untie the financial knots that bound all of them at that time. He was also trying to secure more paying crewmembers. In this quest he had no luck, but he kept battling. Ron's tenacity, despite all their setbacks, was respected by Jeff and the crew.

Ron did make a short excursion into weirdness when he came up with the possibility of an audacious escape plan. He and a couple others cooked it up late one night over drinks. Jeff and the clearer-thinking crew brought them back to reality the next morning. "Sir, should we be successful in making the illegal time-consuming passage out to sea, then what? We would all be branded criminals to be arrested at every port."

Plastered in Brisbane

Finally, *salvation*.

After ninety-seven days of incarceration, and one hundred twenty-two days in the sweltering Port of Brisbane, *Endeavour II* was to be set freed!

On January 28th, 1971, the ship was allowed to depart for New Zealand.

Just how Ron Craig finally accomplished the miracle in freeing his ship was a mystery. For the long months they were stuck in Brisbane, many had thought he was faced with an impossible task. Ron had somehow done it, to his great credit, and the crew were all most thankful that he had succeeded in releasing them from what had come to be regarded by the crew as a hell-hole.

Plastered in Brisbane

To Auckland

A trip to Auckland, New Zealand, should be a simple matter of drawing a straight line on a chart of the Tasman Sea and saying, "Let us shove off!"

It was not so simple in reality. Jeff and Mate Chris Scott studied the best route to sail to Auckland from Brisbane. The weather on the Tasman Sea, as they found, could rise up suddenly to seriously challenge a sailing ship. They had to consider the strong Australia Current, the predominant winds at that time of year, and the possible gales, as well as the need to restock with fuel and water at a midway point like Lord Howe Island. They looked into sailing through Cook Strait to Wellington but that had been deemed notoriously tricky even by Captain Cook. The moniker "Windy Welly" was there for a reason.

> The shimmering Captain hovered over the two, nodding or shaking his head at one decision after the next. A frown of foreboding wrinkled Captain Cook's features as the final route was established.

After much consideration, Jeff and Chris agreed that they would sail around North Cape, North Island and make for Auckland down the more protected eastern shore.

In New Zealand, Ron agreed and began his campaign of searching for investment money. He worked with the single-minded desperation of one who realizes he has this one last chance. All subsequent communications to Jeff were terse and demanding.

Their first day at sea again, and the engineer made a heart-thumping discovery. The only thing worse than finding a foot of water below your bunk would be finding a fire aboard. The engineer detected a small smoldering fire in the engine compartment in a shaft space beside the exhaust. His alarm brought others running with water buckets. They made certain that no further hotspots were in the area then set up a regular watch on the location.

More bad luck on the next day as they found that the newly designed anchor had been badly built by their contractor. It could not be hauled up without a painstaking hours-long process.

Troubles continued on February 1st, near Lord Howe Is., where the engine refused to start. It was repaired and started, after a fashion, but the separate power generator burned out due to salt water seepage.

On top of that, the following day, dirty fuel caused the drive engine to sputter at partial power. Bad luck and over-used equipment and materials were rearing their ugly heads.

Moored at Lord Howe Is., it was determined that neither of the royal sails should be used due to unrepairable hardware issues.

The island was a busy midway point in the sometimes dangerous Tasman. On February 6th, while working on their continuing problems with sails and rigging, they saw two Sunderland flying boats come in for a landing. Jeff had flown before so he was attracted to the grace with which the large machines came down for a water landing.

He commented to a crewman watching beside him, "Our technology has progressed somewhat, from the loose flapping airfoils of our sails, to those lovely machines."

The crewman grinned, "No fun with that, skipper. You just fly over the weather and waves. Where's the excitement?"

"As the Chinese saying goes, beware what you wish for."

Hauling the anchor up that day was a supreme chore again. They motor-sailed for a while as the obstinate contraption was manhandled aboard. With half the crew delegated to the anchor problem, they couldn't set sails.

To Auckland

"Wasted fuel," Jeff muttered to himself.

On the twelfth day at sea from Brisbane, Jeff was asleep in his cabin when Chris banged on his door. It was 0140 hours in the very early morning.

"Skipper, come up! What do you think this is?" as he dragged a waking Jeff up to the night-darkened deck and pointed to the south-south-easterly horizon.

They saw a series of white flares, slowly ascending from the dark surface of the sea, arcing, then winking out. There were at least six of them. Chris said they had seen more before that. Red or white flares at sea indicate serious trouble.

Jeff immediately contacted Wellington Radio, giving the position of the flares. They furled all sail, started the engine and motored to the area, with two hands aloft searching. At 0220 hrs, the lookouts sighted three more white flares. Course was changed to intercept the flares. They spent about twelve hours box-searching without effect. The New Zealand Air Force had sent a four-engined Orion patrol plane, which flew over at 1145. The aircraft reported sighting floating wreckage, but no swimmers or floating bodies.

Air search after big slick seen

An Air Force Orion is searching the Tasman Sea about 240 miles west of New Plymouth after an oil slick "about a mile wide" was reported this morning by an Air New Zealand Electra.

The Orion was diverted from a flight to Ohakea and was over the area about midday.

Earlier the Australian barquentine Endeavour II had reported to Wellington Radio that she had sighted three red flares and one white flare.

The Electra, on a flight from Melbourne, was asked to watch for any signs of a craft in distress.

a.m. that there was an oil slick about a mile in diameter, but said there was no sign at that stage of life or wreckage.

At 9.35 a.m., the Electra descended to investigate what appeared to be wreckage. Captain Owen reported that it seemed to be wood but was unable to positively identify it. The aircraft, with 22 passengers aboard, landed at Wellington an hour late after being earlier delayed at Melbourne by mechanical trouble.

Figure 81 Flares sighted

The *Endeavour II* was released from further searching because their fuel was running low. They were thanked for their good efforts.

Chris muttered to Jeff as they stood down, "Poor bastards. Little chance out here. And, while I certainly do not regret using the fuel for the search, we now have little left for ourselves."

"Not that we can rely on the old diesel. Ever since our previous engineer, Walter Tripp, left, the engine has been falling apart."

Jeff shook his head as he continued, "Mr. Craig has been on about meeting an urgent deadline in Auckland. He did not appreciate our stopping for the S.A.R."

The End

The *Endeavour II* resumed course, sailing in a somewhat crippled fashion to the northern tip of New Zealand.

> Ominous ghosts began to swirl about the ship. One can imagine a titanic battle flashing in the background between Captain Cook and old Neptune himself.
>
> Temporarily flung away by Captain Cook, Neptune flew out of the cabin to morph into an Albatross. The *Angel of Doom* soared persistently, without a wingflap, off the stern of the ship.

Jeff's recollection of an incident at that time was chilling.

> "Two days before we ran into trouble, while we were still north of North Cape, and things seemed difficult but manageable, I was sitting next to the galley drinking a cup of cocoa, gazing out at the sea. It was tempestuous as usual, and the ship was behaving as she normally did. The damn Albatross was still out there, staring at us, waiting.
>
> "Suddenly, a deep foreboding struck me. Out of the blue, this flash of insight and dread told me I was going to lose the ship! Something dreadful was going to happen soon, and all my manoeuvring and efforts could not, or would not, save me from disaster. I knew it was going to happen. However, there was nothing rational to indicate this fate.
>
> "*Endeavour II* was doing as well as she could. The crew was working splendidly. I think that I was doing my job in trying to anticipate and head off potential disasters while meeting Mr. Craig's urgent demands for timeliness in our arrival at Wellington. Yet, now I was struck by this immense, enveloping sense of impending doom. I couldn't tell anyone, for fear I would be

considered to be going 'round the bend'. Logic told me that this was all irrational nerves. I was not getting enough sleep. For months I had faced one challenge after another with this ship, and had usually triumphed. Why not now, I asked myself?"

The intend was to stay forty or fifty miles north of North Cape before sailing down the eastern side of New Zealand's North Island. Every time Jeff radioed Ron Craig in Auckland, Ron entreated him to make haste, for business and publicity reasons. He never ordered, but urged, so he could give the Kiwis a firm estimated time of arrival for the publicity to be prepared.

As in so many disasters, that external pressure of time caused decisions to be made more hastily than they might have otherwise. In looking back, Jeff thought that they may have came about too soon, rounding North Cape before a full forty miles of sea room. It would have taken another twelve hours to fight the winds and current for that extra safety room.

Twelve hours was too long for Ron

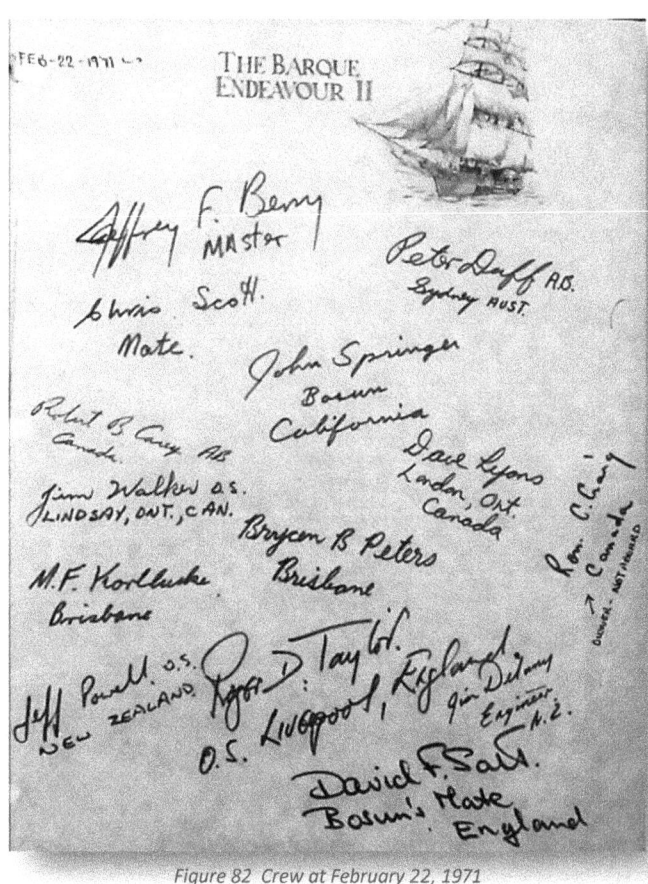

Figure 82 Crew at February 22, 1971

The End

Craig's arrangements in Auckland and Wellington.

On rounding the Cape to start sailing parallel the beach, they faced heavy winds that forced the ship toward the shore. The current had reduced their sea room to only about seven nautical miles. Theoretically, that should have been enough.

Theory went out the window when a starboard chainplate bolt fractured. This slackened the topmast backstay, which sprung the foretopmast. All the pounding that the fore channels had received in the seaway had finally become one too many issues.

Critically, this meant that no sail above the fore course could be set safely on the foremast – only one sail was available on the foremast and its effectiveness was reduced to minimal.

In an instant the *Endeavour II* had been reduced from a handy barque which could tack, wear and sail upwind, into a severely crippled little sailing ship that could not sail upwind. They were limping from then on.

That accursed Albatross stayed to their stern, quietly waiting.

Monday, February 2nd, 1971. The wooden sailing ship was hobbling, making too much leeway and too close to the beach. It was not clear how close they were to shallow water at that time since they were still off the island's shelf.

As a result of the incidents that had occurred since Lord Howe Island, they were almost out of fuel, though it mattered little as the engine might or might not start anyway. All hands were exhausted from the efforts of the previous few days.

> Neptune was rubbing his hands in anticipation. Captain Cook tugged and slapped at the topmast backstay, to no effect. His visage was fading.

The wind was a northeasterly (directly onshore), blowing a steady twenty-five knots, gusting to over thirty-five. In the dark, stormy conditions they could not see ahead. To the stern, the dim light of a

The End

swinging lantern still showed the damn bird following the ship with the disconcerting persistence of a predatory stalker.

The Starboard Watch was Jeff's. At 0105 they were sailing as close to the wind as they possibly could, pushing for a SSE course to keep them off the beach. The night was profoundly dark, with no stars or Moon visible.

At one point, a faint light flashing to starboard was seen and identified as Parengarenga Harbour Light. This gave them a bearing. Jeff had ordered the leadline cast to provide a running measured depth. For each reading, Jeff did a quick calculation by crossing the depth from the chart with the bearing, to give an approximate position. The small anchor forward was catted, ready to drop, and the cable was ranged on deck preparatory to dropping in case it was needed. Jeff had the crew rig a sheet anchor. They shortened the length of the anchor rope so that there was just enough for the anchor to dig in at the bottom, but not enough to allow the ship to swing. As the seaman yelled out the leadline readings, and it showed the depth was changing, they continuously added or took in anchor rope which was secured around the mainmast.

They had only sighted the harbour light through the darkness for perhaps two or three minutes. Sailing on a port tack, the ship made about six knots in the steady wind.

Their first indication of trouble was when the sea suddenly rose up and a wave broke onto the stern, the main deck and along the portside. It wasn't a normal sea wave but a beach type of curling wave. They had sailed into a line of waves, into the surf!

Jeff yelled for all hands. He had the helm down into the wind and the starboard anchor was let go. The ship came up into the wind and stopped. The anchor was dropped but...

 Neptune chortled. Captain Cook screamed silently.

The End

...the anchor chain did not run out beyond the first shackle. The connecting shackle had jammed in the hawse pipe. The anchor was slowly dragging toward the beach.

Jeff ordered the sheet anchor dropped. The Danforth anchor was tipped over the side immediately and this seemed to halt the ship's shoreward movement.

Jeff bellowed, "Drop and furl all sails!" Anything to decrease as much windage aloft as they could.

They were still in the surf line, bounding up and up, rising fifteen to twenty feet, then riding back down. This was reoccurring every minute or so. The ship needed to get out of those waves.

The sheet anchor rode stretched to its full length, then broke suddenly with a loud crack as if Neptune had exploded it with a lightning bolt. The large diameter, supposedly sturdy, polypropylene rope snapped back like a giant rubber band. Its broken end whipped over the rail and demolished things as it went. Six belaying pins with ropes used to control the square sails on the port side were sliced through, as were the lanyards used to stay the main topgallant/royal mast on that side. All were cut apart. Fortunately, nobody was standing in the way of the deadly whip.

At that time Jeff shot off two white parachute flares to try to judge how far they were to shore. The flickering light did not show anything reassuring.

The Mate and Master peered into the night. Jeff pointed, "It's mostly white water and a white beach beyond that, what we can see by this flickering light."

Eerie shadows shimmered against cliffs to the northern side, about a mile off. The crippled ship was tentatively anchored at the entrance of the River Parengarenga, which led to Parengarenga Harbour, about five nautical miles inland. The long, shallow sand ledge was not their friend. Soon, the tide would turn against them, as well.

The End

The ship started dragging again, bouncing twice over the bar into the river's deeper waters, still ploughing a furrow in the sandy bottom. In the deeper water they had to get the big anchor over and into the water immediately.

Jeff yelled to John Springer, "Bosun! Take two men right now to drop the main anchor!"

It took them about two minutes to get the anchor up, its stock mounted, catted and ready to drop. Normally, this took five or six minutes. While Springer was working his men, Scott directed others to flake the anchor chain along the deck so there would be a clear drop. This all happened as the ship was still violently pitching up and down in the swell and waves.

It would be dangerous to drop the big anchor under these conditions, with the most touchy part being veering the cable to allow it to dig in.

Jeff ordered everyone to climb onto the galley roof then he went to the braided nylon and gingerly took off two turns, standing back six feet before slowly slackening the rope. It almost instantly grew tight around the Sampson post from the strain. Jeff wanted to ease out enough rope to stop *Endeavour II* from going aground.

The third time he eased the anchor rode, it got away from him, happening lightning fast so that he couldn't react. Instinctively, he hung onto the rope but that pulled his right hand and forearm around the post for one complete turn. Jeff's forearm felt as if it had suddenly been put into a fire. Even then, with his left arm he was able to control the rope and clap a tugboat hitch on it around the Sampson post to stop it from running out any more.

This stopped the ship from immediate grounding so that they were no longer bumping shoreward.

Jeff's right forearm was badly broken, dangling uselessly. The engineer, a former Australian Army combat medic, treated him. He knocked apart a wooden crate and manufactured a set of splints for the arm. Then he pulled the bones back into place and bound

The End

everything tightly. He asked if there was any cloth to make a sling for the arm. As they were in the galley when he asked, Jeff sent for the ship's old Canadian flag in the Chart Room. It worked well as a sling.

No one else was hurt. The ship was as secure as one could expect, held by two anchors. They were facing directly stern towards the beach, bow to the sea. The ship rode the sea more comfortably in this manner.

Jeff went to the radio to send a Mayday signal. "Mayday mayday may..." he started.

"Get off this frequency! We're listening for distress signals!"

Jeff looked at the mic as if it had turned into a sausage.

He flipped the frequency knob and finally made contact with Radio Awanui and Auckland Radio.

"Yes, a mayday! Our ship is the barque *Endeavour II* in dire condition, with fourteen souls aboard, anchored in surf off the beach at Parengarenga Harbour. Need immediate assistance!"

In reply he heard the all too common Kiwi reply to problems, "She'll be right, Skipper. We'll send help."

The engineer was ordered to try to start the engine so they could motor as far seaward as they could. The old engine did sputter to life, barely. All oil lamps were ordered collected and drained of their kerosene, and that fuel dribbled into the engine's day tank. It was a desperate move but even that was not enough.

Throughout the early morning hours, Jeff was constantly in (one-handed) communication with various New Zealand governmental authorities. He asked for a tugboat and at least a launch to bring them fuel. They wanted to know how many people were on board, how many injured, and how many animals. When Jeff admitted they had a cat, the bureaucrats took immediate umbrage.

The End

The bureaucrats were now in full speed. It prompted a quick call from a man with a very Irish brogue, reminding Jeff that under no circumstances would the cat be allowed ashore. Jeff told him dryly that they had more pressing things to consider at that exact moment, like surviving a shipwreck.

The grounded ship was promised a tugboat from Doubtless Bay, which would depart immediately and be alongside by daybreak. It looked as though they might be able to save the ship.

Day broke to a stormy sea with a gale-force onshore wind and high to moderate surf. However, no tugboat came. Finally, Jeff received a call saying that, unfortunately, the tug would not be arriving, since it had sailed out of the harbour, hit some waves, and decided it was too dangerous to venture any farther.

"But, she'll be right, Skipper. Just hang on."

Jeff gathered up all the legal and important documents, charts, etc., to be stowed in a waterproofed chest. A smaller army ammunition box was used for the cameras, watches and a few other valuables. The propane cooking gas bottles were turned off for safety.

They brought the two life rafts down from the Galley roof to the stern and laid them out. One was in a fibreglass canister. The other was in a canvas satchel. All the life jackets were gathered. Jeff made sure that everyone had one jacket to wear, and then they tied themselves together with one line and put one extra life jacket between each person. That way, Jeff ensured they would be able to reach one for additional flotation. Most of the crew wore U.S. Navy inflatable jackets, which had been scrounged from the Navy back in Bremerton Naval Base the year before.

As he thought about it, Jeff mumbled, "These better inflate."

By 9 am the wooden ship had become the local entertainment, with people lining up on the beach, even in the heavy wind. Some were looking and pointing, others were riding prancing horses back and

The End

forth. The press corps was gathering, recording the whole scene. Soon several olive-drab Landrovers arrived and parked on the sand. They were followed by New Zealand Army lorries parking next to them. Within an hour or so, a row of four or five Army bell tents had sprung up on the beach. One had a Red Cross flag flapping heavily from its front entrance. The onshore gale buffeted the tents and kicked up swirling dervishes of sand.

On the *Endeavour II*, the wet and exhausted crew were holding tightly onto and around the galley roof, amazed at the spectacle on shore. The Kiwis had turned their emergency into a jolly good civil defence drill! However, no one had thought to bring boats to save them or to deliver diesel fuel, as requested.

An hour later they spotted a small motor launch trying to fight its way out of Parengarenga Harbour. It had a drum of fuel prominently loaded on the foredeck. Neptune's gale was still too strong for the boat and it was forced to turn and retreat back into the bay.

Desperately working on shore, Ron Craig had done his damnedest to help. He had been in the launch during that attempt at delivering fuel. It was a brave but futile gesture. The weather continued to try to batter the ship ashore, with gale force of forty to fifty knots.

Nothing was working. The engine was lit, sputtering, to charge the battery, taking the fuel down to a vapour.

The tide turned sometime before noon. Now ebbing, it swung the ship around so it faced northwestward. Since the water under her keel was decreasing every minute, the angle of each anchor chain was decreasing. This meant that the angle of the chains became almost parallel with the beach gradient. When the tide ebbed, that slack pulled the *Endeavour II* around. She had started out facing the sea. When the tide turned, she ended up pointing northerly, turning 90-degree to port. In doing so, she fouled one of the anchor rodes around her rudder assembly at the stern, anchoring her by the bow with one anchor, and by the stern with the other anchor. They were

The End

lying broadside to the sea, taking the full brunt of the gale winds, unable to move on her own.

Eventually, time and tide and water ran out. The ship bounced on the bottom. At first it was a thump, then a harder belt, then a strong rattling whack on the keel, which shivered all the way up the rigging, shaking the spars. As the water went out from under her, flotation and stability went with it. *Endeavour II* heeled over onto her portside bilge, lying at about a 45-degree angle. In all, once she had taken the sand, she did not move about. The hull was not initially damaged; however, now that it was motionless, the hull took shuddering blows with each wave.

Head bowed, cap in hand, Captain Cook faded away.

Neither did the *Endeavour II* help her crew by fully beaching herself. To leave the ship, the crew would still be in treacherous waters. Extra heavy waves smashed into the wooden vessel periodically and ripped away parts. If the crew were to drop into the water under those conditions they could be sucked under the ship, taken out to sea, battered against the ship, or all of the above.

By this time, all hands were around the helm at the stern. Jeff give a speech that was the hardest any master has to give.

"I am sorry that I got you into this mess. However, I still think that if we can cut the anchor rode, which is snagged around the rudder, and get a tow of about two hundred yards, the ship should survive. Meanwhile, we will have to abandon it sooner or later, then I hope to come back with help.

"You have been a great crew. All of you. It has been my greatest honour to be your skipper. I hope we still have many sea miles together ahead of us.

"Now, let's all keep cool heads, not take any unnecessary chances and all of us help our shipmates.

The End

"Thank you all for your great work and effort on *Monte Cristo/Endeavour II*. Good Luck!"

For once, there was no talkback or argument from anyone. Each crewman did exactly as instructed.

The dreaded *abandon ship* preparations needed to be started.

Their main lifeboat, called a painter, was made ready and the backup raft was inflated. In the midst of that work, a heavy wave from the surf swept across the deck taking the painter and raft away from the soaked crew, sweeping the painter away and under the stern. Lines from the inflatable were captured and secured. But before anyone could yell about the painter, the brand new lifeboat, with its canopy proudly covering empty seats and all the survival equipment, was taken away by the wind toward the shore, eventuality to be beached. People ashore ran to it, expecting to save someone but they shouted in surprise that it was empty.

The remaining lifeboat was an eight-foot inflatable that had been used back in Canada. Jeff prayed that it would now hold together in their real-life test.

The skipper gave the command to *Abandon Ship*, and slowly, carefully, all hands slipped into the water one at a time. There was rigging hanging everywhere. John Springer got his feet caught on something and panicked for a moment until another crewman dove down to free him. In the water, the waves tossed them about until the ship's master, last of all, slipped in. The waves and current captured the group, taking them under *Endeavour II*'s rigging. Staying together, they drifted toward the bow.

Vicky Watts, the only female aboard, had fainted soon after she entered the water. She was held above water until Jeff and others who were then in the raft could drag her into it. They made sure any of the others were pulled in if they needed the help. The rest of the crew circled the raft, tied together. They floated, concentrating on keeping their heads above water in the slapping waves.

The End

A sound heard over the waves was John Springer moaning, over and over, "Oh, our beautiful barque! Our beautiful barque! Oh God, our beautiful *Endeavour II!*" That sentiment was in everyone's mind.

As part of their preparation, Jeff had ordered the crew to dress warmly, so the water temperature, while chilly, did not affect them. Nevertheless, the waves and surf tossed them about relentlessly. Every five to ten minutes Jeff did a head count to ensure that all hands were still together.

It took a full hour of surf bouncing before their feet touched sand and they were able to wade. Looking back when they could, they saw their ship had stranded slightly less than a mile offshore. The hull was still intact.

Wading dejectedly through the waves toward North Island, New Zealand, they were finally met by three Auckland police officers, complete with London bobby-style helmets, who waded into the water all the way up to their ankles. A news photographer covered all this. The next day there was a picture in The Auckland Star of "The *Endeavour II* crew being rescued by members of the Auckland Police".

When the crew saw that they couldn't believe it. "Instead of posing for pictures, why didn't anyone get us a boat or fuel?"

Ron Craig met the crew as they waded ashore. The devastated owner was much the worse for wear, and was crying at the meeting. Jeff's and Ron's emotions poured forth as they fell into each other's arms.

The crew were ushered into the Red Cross tent where medics checked each of them out. In shock from both his broken arm and the loss of the *Endeavour II*, Jeff was manic, asking for assistance for his ship.

The End

"The ship needs urgent attention! Get a tug out to her!"

But nobody was listening.

The stoic New Zealand response was no more than a pat on the head.

Figure 83 Endeavour II in the surf of Parengarenga Bay

After being checked out, they were driven to a nearby farmhouse for a shower and dry clothes. Distracted, Jeff had left his 35mm film canisters in the bathroom but never saw them again. Also noted by the crew was the fact that the majority of the clothing they were given to change into came from stores that had been lying around for shipwrecked seamen. These were fifty years or more out of date.

The End

Later, they were taken back to the beach and to the tent with the Red Cross. Jeff was given a needle. He woke up in a hospital in Kaitaia, the town nearest to the wreck site. The short rest gave them back some energy. Jeff and others demanded to go back to see the ship. Someone drove them onto the beach.

By then, the dazzling white beach outside of Parengarenga Bay was bathed in bright sunlight. There was scarcely a cloud in the sky.

Capt. J. F. Berry, master of the Endeavour, with his arm in a sling followed by the first mate, Mr C. Scott, leaving the house in Te Kao where they received hot food and drinks after coming ashore from the wreck.

Figure 84 *Skipper Jeff Berry with a fresh sling*

Jeff, properly bandaged with a sling for his arm, asked a police officer on duty at the wreck site, "What has happened to our ship? Has it been secured?"

The officer shook his head, "Afraid not, mate. Wave after wave hit her, broke her into bits."

The End

Focusing out on the sand in the distance, they could see the *Endeavour II* smashed into her constituent parts.

They walked for a mile on the sand, then further, passing planks and rigging strung out for another couple miles. The bow had held together but someone had sawn off the figurehead. The white sand was dotted with what appeared to be coins. These would be the ten tons of steel boiler punchings that had been installed as ballast in San Francisco.

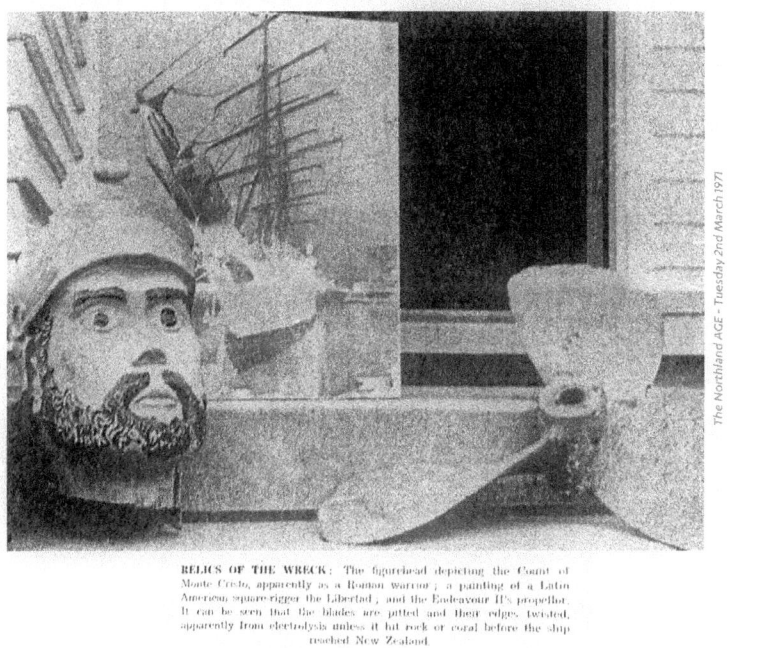

Figure 85 from the Northland ACE

In a disbelieving daze, they wandered through the wreckage, shaking their heads in shock. The crew soon found that there was not one single salvageable thing remaining. All the canned food, tools, clothing and personal effects had disappeared. Of course, the

The End

authorities denied that any looting had taken place. That explanation could be understandable, until it happened to oneself, personally.

Rigging and even larger sections of the ship had gone walkabout, as the Australian crew members remarked wryly.

Figure 86 Leftovers

Portions of the ship can still be found in the local museum, Te Ahu Heritage Museum, Kaitaia, Northland, New Zealand.

As with any major disaster, an inquiry was held. The circumstances leading up to the end of the *Monte Cristo/Endeavour II* were thoroughly reviewed. No blame was assigned.

While each member of the crew and the owner were devastated, she was gone. They were left with their own memories, each with their own perspective.

Then they moved on.

Figure 87 Thanks to Don Hammond, Curator-Manager, Te Ahu Heritage Museum. Holding a deadeye, with a section of Endeavour II rail on the table.

Figure 88 the end

The End

The End

Ronald C. Craig

Monte Cristo/Endeavour II Owner, lost everything in the wreck. He found another decaying sailing ship in the United States and tried mightily to get her up and going. He was defeated as a result of the previous owner not standing by the agreement of sail that was made so that venture ultimately had to be abandoned. After his sailing ship adventures, Ron picked himself up and made another fortune. He retired to Rancho Mirage, California, near the home of the late comedian Bob Hope.

Ron died on January 15, 2009, and is missed by many who remember his sometimes outlandish, larger than life antics (such as dressing as the Count of Monte Cristo, and Captain James Cook) and unusual business projects. He left behind many friends and family who will never forget him. One of his favorite expressions, "I'll tell you one thing and that's not two." His grandchildren loved that.

The End

Jeff Berry

Master of *Monte Cristo-Endeavour II*, worked as a journalist in New Zealand for a year after the shipwreck. He moved to Tahiti, where he became assistant editor of an English language magazine there. In 1973, he resumed his nautical career, journeying to England where he participated in the building and sailing of the replica galleon *Golden Hinde*. He later served as her mate and finally as master. Jeff was skipper of the ship when it was featured in Japan, in the filming of *Shogun*. He was master subsequently of the full-rigged ship *Cruz del Sur*, the brig *Unicorn*, the barquentine *Osprey*, and several motor vessels. He moved to China, where he built yachts and was a marine surveyor. Jeff spent time in Singapore, where he wrote and taught school.

Jeff presently resides in Olympia, Washington, where he is writing several books that are the history of his remarkable family and his own travels, starting with the Rutherford Press title, **Notes To Mother**.

The End

Ron M. Craig

Mate of the *Monte Cristo*, and co-author.

Ron Marion Craig (Ron Jr). Born in Edmonton Alberta Canada and named after both mother and father. Could hardly believe his eyes when he first saw the *Monte Cristo*. And to sail on her! Wow – that was a thrill, even though it was a short time. I say now I wish I had stayed on board but at an early age it was tough to decide life's ways. My father had always wanted a book about his adventures, so here it is, Pop.

Ron Jr resides with his wife, a successful Beauty Salon owner, and granddaughter, Aleka.

Ron is working in the advertising field in Northern British Columbia. He loves sports, and after a stint in acting in 2016, with a part in the Award winning Canadian film *Hello Destroyer* and the documentary *Moving Back in all Directions*, about The Doors, would like to add acting to his hobbies, play golf and retire some day.

The End

Look for our special feature – more pictures and information, all on our website:

https://rutherfordpress.ca/in-a-cloud-of-sails/

And check out Ron's Facebook site:

https://www.facebook.com/Monte-Cristo-Endeavour-11-1474516472771354/

Figure 89 On the Yard, in better days

The End

Figures

Figure 1 Alex Brigola 2
Figure 2 Hull under construction, January 1967 4
Figure 3 The Albatross, from http://de.academic.ru/dic.nsf/dewiki/45845 7
Figure 4 The barque Monte Cristo under full sail 8
Figure 5 Under construction 10
Figure 6 Shareholder Certificate 10
Figure 7 Rolling toward the shore, next to the Second Narrows Crossing 11
Figure 8 from Rules for Classification and Construction Ship Technology:
http://www.gl-group.com/infoServices/rules/pdfs/gl_i-4-1_e.pdf 12
Figure 9 Joe Klausner 13
Figure 10 Painting the hull 14
Figure 11 Brigola's notes on sailing 15
Figure 12 The ship drew visitors 17
Figure 13 Port & starboard sides of the main cabin 18
Figure 14 Figurehead, carved by Brigola 19
Figure 15 Another ship? 21
Figure 16 Monte Cristo / Endeavour II 22
Figure 17 Capt. James Cook - statue in Victoria's Inner Harbour, British Columbia ... 25
Figure 18 1970 – Ron C. Craig in Australia, before a painting of Capt. James Cook 26
Figure 19 Docked at Mosquito Creek (see it?) 27
Figure 20 Crew Aloft 28
Figure 21 Monte Cristo brochure 29
Figure 22 Monte Cristo Charter Line USA registration 30
Figure 23 Berth at Bayshore Inn, Vancouver 30
Figure 24 Welcomed at the Bayshore Inn, Vancouver 31
Figure 25 "Brothers Fore" 35
Figure 26 Ron Sr. aloft 36

Figure 27   Gale on Georgia Strait, Nanaimo Free Press 42

Figure 28   Ron Jr. at the helm, in front of Capt. Gilchrist, on English Bay, Vancouver 43

Figure 29 Ron Jr. - Rope work 44

Figure 30   Starboard view 46

Figure 31   Early crew – 1969 – with Ron Craig Sr. at the wheel..................... 47

Figure 32   Vancouver Archives – "CVA 447-7004.2 - Sailing Ship Montecristo".......... 48

Figure 33   Becoming seamen 49

Figure 34 Ralph Eastland in the high rigging, with Luis Dammert below: Seattle Times 50

Figure 35 Fred Craig and passenger, Powell River 53

Figure 36   Action commenced in June 1969 54

Figure 37   Monte Cristo Charter Line crest 55

Figure 38   The crew, prior to sailing to the USA, 1969 56

Figure 39   Ballast time 57

Figure 40   The Calipso at Lake Union Dry Dock... 59

Figure 41   Request to join the crew 59

Figure 42   Captured by the New Jersey 60

Figure 43   Captain Peniston and Ron C. Craig... 61

Figure 44   Crew Aloft 63

Figure 45   Seattle Times July 1969 65

Figure 46   Promotion brochure 68

Figure 47   Motoring, with canvas flapping 70

Figure 48 Approaching San Francisco 74

Figure 49   Ron Sr. as Captain Cook 77

Figure 50   San Francisco – sails are finally ship-shape................................. 78

Figure 51   Monte Cristo, port side 83

Figure 52   from Alcatraz! Alcatraz! by Adam Fortunate Eagle 84

Figure 53   from article by Tim Findley, San Francisco Examiner 90

Figure 54   Media coverage - San Francisco Examiner 91

Figure 55   Article by Tim Findley, San Francisco Examiner.......................... 92

Figure 56   Myrt - from a sketch by Loreena M. Lee...................................... 97

Figures

Figure 57 Skipper Jeff 98
Figure 58 Larry's new spanker sail 103
Figure 59 Release from further legal action 113
Figure 60 On the Pacific 117
Figure 61 Below deck 121
Figure 62 from "Captain Cook" map, http://www.history-map.com/ 123
Figure 63 The goal: Tahiti, Feb. 1970 128
Figure 64 The little deck cannon 129
Figure 65 from "la Depeche de Tahiti" 130
Figure 66 from "The Tahiti Bulletin" 131
Figure 67 Brando allowed few pictures at that time 132
Figure 68 The Sirens Called 136
Figure 69 from Fiji Times. Coincidences. 146
Figure 70 The Russians Are Coming! 147
Figure 71 Picture by the Royal Australian Air Force 149
Figure 72 from the Sydney Sun 154
Figure 73, the ship's sponsor, The Sydney Morning Herald 155
Figure 74 Ron Craig and bewigged Jeff Berry, Mate Thomas with Tero Raa 156
Figure 75 In Sydney, from government tourist info 160
Figure 76 from Wikipedia, "Tasman Sea" 165
Figure 77 Postal proof 166
Figure 78 Bustard Head Lighthouse - per News Corp Australia 170
Figure 79 Brisbane crew 171
Figure 80 Endeavour II in Australia 174
Figure 81 Flares sighted 179
Figure 82 Crew at February 22, 1971 182
Figure 83 Endeavour II in the surf of Parengarenga Bay 193
Figure 84 Skipper Jeff Berry with a fresh sling 194
Figure 85 from the Northland ACE 195
Figure 86 Leftovers 196
Figure 87 Thanks to Don Hammond, Curator-Manager, Te Ahu Heritage Museum. 197

Figures

Figure 88 the end 197

Figure 89 On the Yard, in better days..202

Pictures taken by the crew are presented here "in the raw"

Copyright permissions as noted, or assigned to the authors

www.ingramcontent.com/pod-product-compliance
Lightning Source LLC
Chambersburg PA
CBHW051558010526
44118CB00023B/2743